SURVIVOR

SURVIVOR

MEMOIRS OF A PROSTITUTE

MARTINA KEOGH WITH JEAN HARRINGTON

MAVERICK HOUSE PUBLISHERS

Published by Maverick House,
Unit 115 Ashbourne Industrial Estate,
Ashbourne, Co. Meath.
info@maverickhouse.com
http://www.maverickhouse.com

First published in 2003
(This edition third reprint)

ISBN 0-9542945-4-8

The rights of the authors have been asserted.

Martina dedicates the book to
her brothers, sisters, daughter and grandchildren for
their love and support.

Jean dedicates the book to
the loving memory of her father Robert.

Acknowledgments

Martina Keogh

There are a lot of people who have contributed to this book in one way or another so a big thank you to those people. I'd like to thank the following: Sister Fiona Pryle for her support and friendship, and for inspiring me to tell my story; Berna Egar for her friendship and kindness; Sergeant Martina Noonan and Detective Sergeant Jo O'Leary for showing great kindness and humanity.

The following people helped both my mental and physical health throughout the years and I'm thankful to them: Gerardine, Jennifer and all at Ruhama; Mary and Deirdre from the Women's Health Project; Sisters Nattie, Gemma and Helena gave me great support and kindness over the years. Thanks to Garda Stephen Bell for his support, and to the late Fr. John O'Sullivan for being a good friend; also to Kitty.

I have been blessed with great friends and family, and I'd like to thank them all deeply. You know who you are.

Thanks to my loyal friend and neighbour, Alice, for all that you've done. Florence has always been a very good friend to me and she gives me enormous help with my animal rescue; I couldn't do it without you. I'd like to thank Frank who gave me the inspiration and courage to write this, and whom I sadly miss since he passed away. His daughters Sue and Pauline remain good friends of mine. Thanks also to Melda from Cut Price Gold for being a good friend to my family over the years. Finally, thanks to my beautiful daughter for her love, kindness, and support throughout the years.

Jean Harrington

As with any project of this magnitude, there are a lot of people who have helped me along the way. I am eternally grateful for their support.

I'd like to add my thanks to Sister Fiona Pryle, without whom this book would not have been written. A big thanks to Martina Keogh for sharing her personal story with me. I'd like to thank everyone who clarified details including Superintendent Derek Byrne, the staff of Ruhama, and solicitor Garret Sheehan. Thanks to Focus Ireland for supplying me with literature.

Thanks to my good friend Corina Cummins for transcribing interviews in my hour of need and for editing the manuscript so well. I'm also blessed to have friends such as Alan Faherty, Gillian Galvin, Helen Walsh, Caitríona Prestage, Catherine O'Reilly, Orlagh Uí Mhuineóg, Áine Ní Chonghaíle, Sinéad O'Neill, Áine Nic Gabhann and Jackie Conlon.

To my mother, Aveen, who is a truly beautiful and selfless lady. Her passion for learning and reading inspired a love of books in me and for that I thank her deeply. My late father, Robert, was my finest critic / proofreader and helped immeasurably with my writing. I'd like to honour him posthumously for his love and direction. My sisters and brothers, Ann, Susie, Robert, and Martin encouraged me all the way. Thanks for your love. A huge thanks to Mary and Richie for taking such good care of my daughter, Aoileann, while I finished the book.

Finally there is the love of my life, John, who inspires me. Thank you so much.

INTRODUCTION

Introduction

One evening when I was in my early twenties and walking across Baggot Street Bridge, a car pulled up beside me. I thought the driver was lost and leaned towards the car to offer directions. The young man driving asked if I was working. I fell back from the car saying a shocked but firm 'no', and walked quickly off. He followed me along the road driving very slowly, and it was only when it appeared that I was making a call on my mobile phone that he drove off.

I was wearing jeans and a coat during this incident. I couldn't believe he could mistake me for a prostitute. Me—a hooker? I imagined all prostitutes wore fishnet stockings, leather clothing and hung around street corners. They didn't stride purposefully down the street, as far as I was aware.

I felt violated and vulnerable, and I knew that man could have easily dragged me off in his car had he so desired. It got me thinking about the type of woman who worked on the streets. What would possess a woman to expose herself to the threat of violence on a regular basis? Was there more than one type of woman; what kind of men crawled the streets looking for them? Did the women always do it for the money, or were there other reasons which forced them to sell their bodies?

I never expected some years later, that I would befriend someone who had worked as a prostitute and get all my questions answered. They were rarely, however, the answers I expected.

.   .   .

I was researching a book on vice when I heard about Martina through a mutual friend. I had been talking to various prostitutes and professionals involved in the sex industry. Martina's life story sounded tragically fascinating and I was intrigued by it. I was told she wanted to write a book, but needed someone to interpret her experiences, so we decided to see if we could strike up a working relationship.

We spoke on the phone and she invited me to her flat to meet for the first time. I was struck by Martina's willingness to let me into her life. I don't know many people who would invite a stranger into their home, but she was very welcoming.

Her flat was crammed with cats, Yorkshire terriers, stuffed turtles, and kitschy lights. It was warm and cosy, and housed a few dogs that she fostered.

She welcomed me into her personal space to talk about the most intimate and most tragic moments of her life.

I soon realised that it was a clever idea. While I initially interpreted it as a sign that she was trusting and open, I quickly became aware I was on her territory and her domain, which was exactly what she wanted.

This is the way she has led her life both privately and professionally. She has a way about her that lets people assume what they want, but she's always the one in control. She is astute and clever, witty and streetwise. She's also tough, strong, and soft.

I spent many hours with Martina in her flat learning about her life and experiences. She told me how she became a streetwalker, and about her life as a prostitute. She remained a prostitute for 30 years before she eventually found a way out. I learned about the netherworld of prostitution through her eyes; a world where trust is abused and human life has little value. We recorded hours of conversation over two years and spent many more hours talking while we strolled around Dublin.

From the beginning I became immersed in her world. She introduced me to her madam—the woman who sold her services when she was just eight years old. We went to Ruhama (a voluntary organisation that works with women in prostitution) and looked at some paintings she had done. We had a couple of adventures of our own during the nights we drove around Dublin.

Her story is tragic and painful; entertaining and interesting. She's honest to a fault when it comes to detailing how she's behaved in the past. I wondered why she would want people to know all she's been through and everything she has done, now that she no longer works in the sex industry.

When I asked her why she wanted her story told, she said she knew she had an extraordinary tale to tell. People often told her she should write a book but she didn't know how to do it. She knew that she would have to meet someone who would be willing to write it for her. When I contacted her asking to meet, the time was right.

Although it is a true story, I have changed the names of all the women in the book to protect their privacy. Martina is writing under her own name.

· · ·

This book is written through Martina's voice. They are her memories of the life she has lived and the streets she walked. Any inaccuracies in detail are simply because they are her interpretations of events.

Survivor is the memoir of Martina's life. Such is the basis of memoirs. It is not a biography detailing dates and times. Her memoirs will never achieve the objectivity that a biography would, and lacks some of the impartiality and distance that a biographer might have.

Martina can only tell us about her secret world from her line of vision. Through her we are able to see how the prostitute views her clients and how much money she turns over. We see how the prostitute interacts with the police and how the law treated her. We are allowed a glimpse of a world that usually remains sordidly and secretly out of bounds.

It is primarily a story of human interest—one that is continuing beyond the pages of this book—for Martina and the other prostitutes who are still walking the streets.

Jean Harrington
August 2003

MARTINA'S STORY

Prologue

I never aspired to become a prostitute. I can't remember what I wanted to be when I was growing up. If I had a choice, I would have probably liked to become a vet, but I knew I didn't have many choices. I always loved animals and spent most of my youth rescuing stray and abandoned animals. They were always a source of comfort, and were affectionate to me when no one else was. Even today my house is always full of dogs, cats, and strays that I pick up. I have an empathy with animals that I never had with humans and they always seemed to like me.

Today I make a living by working as a cleaner. I always made an honest wage for myself. I'm not ashamed of the fact that I was a prostitute. I'm proud that I was able to look after my daughter and myself without resorting to crime. It really drives me crazy when I hear people excoriate prostitutes. They rarely mention the men who use them.

The simple fact of the matter is that prostitutes wouldn't exist if men didn't pay for sex. Men initiate the encounter; men pay for it. They are the ones who choose to leave their loved ones while they seek pleasure and satisfaction elsewhere. The women are only there because they have no choice. They work as prostitutes because they need the money, and most of them believe they have no other way of making money. I believed this for years. I thought my life would always be this way; I couldn't see a way out, but out of nowhere a path appeared. I took the path away from prostitution and have never looked back.

No woman grows up wanting to work as a prostitute. It is a choice that we make when the choices are limited; when it appears there is no other option. It is a way of making a living that doesn't hurt anyone except the woman herself. As I child I had never heard the term prostitute. Ironically—tragically—although I had never heard the term, I was already working as one. I started in prostitution when I was just eight years old. I turned to prostitution as a means to survive.

. . .

I was born out of wedlock. Although it's a common occurrence nowadays, back in the fifties it brought great shame on my mother's family. She was raised in a strict household and parish in Co. Kerry. My grandmother was a severe Russian woman and a devout Catholic. My grandfather was a schoolteacher and they were well respected in the community. An unmarried, pregnant daughter was unthinkable.

My mother, Maureen, was going out with a Belfast man, Val, at the time. When she realised she was pregnant, she couldn't face telling her parents, so she ran away with Val to England. My older brother, Peter, was born and they lived in England as a family. They were, by all accounts, very happy together. They never got married because he was a Protestant and she was a Catholic, but they were left in peace when they lived in England. Apparently my grandparents were happy enough with this arrangement because my parents were far enough away to stop the neighbours prying.

Then my mother got pregnant with me. I sometimes think about destiny and how mine might have been different if my father hadn't been killed at such a young age. Because it was raining heavily, he lost control of the car he was driving; he didn't survive the crash. Although I was still in my mother's womb, his death changed my life. Maureen was only 19 years old and wasn't able to cope with the tragedy of losing her partner while rearing two young children, so she gave Peter to her parents to look after for a while. They never knew she was pregnant with me and she kept it that way. I don't know why; whatever her reasons were, I was her secret. After Val died she moved back to Ireland. Peter was living with my grandparents in Kerry and she got a job in Dublin city. I was born in the Coombe Maternity Hospital on a sunny summer's day and my mother's heart broke.

She wasn't able to keep me and work, so my mother gave me to a woman who said that she would take care of me until my mother could take me back. This worked out well for a few months. My mother sent the woman money for my keep and came to visit me as often as she could. One day when she arrived to see me the woman claimed she was keeping me for herself. My mother was horrified. She got in touch with the police who had me returned to her.

After this experience she sent me to a children's home in Kilkenny where everything was above board. She paid my way while she got herself settled in Dublin. One day she determined she could have me back in her life and she sent for me.

.   .   .

The children's home was great. My memories of it consist of just images really. I remember playing in a sand pit with some of the other children; and my best friend was a girl called Caroline. There were red gingham tablecloths in the dining room and we had jelly and ice cream for dessert every day. There were cats there and I loved playing with their kittens.

I was four years old when they put me on a train to Dublin. Mrs. Carroll, the supervisor, gave me a lollipop and told me I was going to see my Mammy and live with her. I didn't really know what she was talking about, because I had no memory of seeing my mother. Most of the children were orphans, but a few of them knew they had parents somewhere. I didn't mind going on the train on my own because I had sandwiches and a yogurt in my bag for when I got hungry. The sandwiches were my favourite kind— cheese and ham. The train travelled quickly and I liked passing the time by watching the cows and sheep in the fields.

After I ate my sandwiches, I fell asleep. When I woke up the train was pulling into a station and everyone started to get their bags. I stayed where I was because I didn't know what was going on.

The train suddenly blew its horn; people were laughing and talking above the noise. I was very frightened by the noises and strange surroundings. The conductor came over to me.

'Come on, love,' he said. 'Let's get you over to your Mammy.'

He took my hand and we got off the train. There were bags on the platform and steam was coming from the train. I'd never seen so many people in my life. The conductor led me through the crowd. There was a woman standing behind barriers wearing a long, grey coat. She walked towards me and hunched down to wrap her arms around me.

'My baby Martina,' she said. 'I've missed you so much. You're home now. You're home with your Ma.'

Her coat was rough and her brown hair got in my eyes, but she wouldn't let go of me. Eventually she got up and took my bag from the ground. I didn't want her to take it, but she didn't notice and brought me towards the barrier. I looked for the conductor. I wanted to tell him to bring me back to Mrs. Carroll and my friends in Kilkenny but he was gone; lost in the crowd. I didn't see him after that.

The woman—my mother—started talking to a man who was holding onto a pram. I tried to look into the pram but I wasn't big enough to see inside. I could only make out a few white blankets. A big boy stood beside it staring at me.

My mother put her arm around the man and said, 'This is your Daddy.' She stood behind the boy and gently pushed him towards me.

'This is your brother, Peter, and your sister Margaret is asleep in the pram. Peter, this is Martina, your little sister.'

I wondered what she was talking about. I didn't have any brothers and sisters. I always thought I was an orphan, just like my friend Caroline. That's what she told me. I wanted to go back to Kilkenny. I wanted to be with my friends; not these strangers who called themselves my family.

We walked out of the train station onto the street. It was freezing cold, but the woman—my mother—grabbed my hand and we walked very quickly. We crossed over a bridge and I saw my first glimpse of the River Liffey. I thought it was the sea because it looked so big to me.

'Look, it's the sea,' I said. With that my mother laughed genially and said, 'No, Martina. It's the River Liffey, but it leads to the sea eventually. Can you see those seagulls? That's where they'll fly to later on.' I watched the seagulls and wished I could fly out to sea with them.

We continued walking until we got to a big building, which we entered. Some of the stairs were broken and we had to be careful not to fall. Mam lifted Margaret and the man pushed the pram into a corner under the stairs. Mam said, 'Peter, hold Martina's hand going up them stairs.'

Peter looked sulky. I didn't like him and I didn't want him to take my hand, but he took it firmly and we walked up the stairs. Up, up and up we went for what seemed like an eternity. We stepped around rags with dirt on them and avoided the broken steps. We stopped outside a door and my new father opened it.

The room was very dark. A pair of curtains hung from the window, blocking most of the light. There was a big bed under the window and a cot at the end of it. The other side of the room had a sink and a cooker. There was a fireplace opposite the door, and a table in the middle of the room. Mam put Margaret in the cot.

'Welcome home, Martina. This is where you're going to be living now. Welcome to Yorke Street in the fair city of Dublin.'

She came over and started to take off my coat, but I could feel the tears welling up in my eyes. I started to cry and I couldn't stop. I pulled away from her.

'I want to go home! I want to go home! I don't like it here!'

I ran to the door and started screaming and banging to get out. I wanted to get out of there—to go home to Kilkenny—or anywhere really. I got hysterical and started to hiccup until I felt a clatter across my head. I stopped suddenly and looked around to see my mother with her face flushed red and her hair tossed. Gone was the woman who was hugging me and calling me her baby.

'Martina, stop being such a little bitch! You're home now. There is nowhere to go. This is where you're going to stay. Now shut up and be quiet!'

I spent the rest of the night whimpering, but remembered what would happen if I started crying again, so I didn't raise my voice for the rest of the night.

chapter one

The first few weeks in my strange new home passed in a blur. I was only four years old, yet I had a survival instinct that told me I had to keep quiet and do what I was asked if I didn't want to get slapped around. That really marked the end of my carefree youth. From then on, I had a thoroughly miserable childhood. I shudder every time I think about it.

My mother used to wreck the place. She had such a vicious temper and she would lose it very easily. She'd smash everything around her—plates, cups, saucers—it didn't matter what she had in her hands; she would just throw it towards the door when she was angry.

The only carefree childhood I had known was down in the children's home before my mother brought me home to Dublin. I was allowed to be a child in Kilkenny, but I had to grow up very quickly living with Mam and my stepfather, Paddy. Although he wasn't my real father, I called him Dad from the day I met him.

My mother was very beautiful. She had big brown eyes with long lashes and a petite frame. She was a lovely woman in many ways. There were times when she sat brushing my hair and telling me I was a beautiful little girl. She loved children and she often took in children who needed a break from their family home. She fostered lots of children unofficially. Everybody liked her and she is still spoken well of to this day.

It's hard to talk about her, however, without remembering how she used to beat me around the place. Now that I'm older and a mother myself, I can attain some clarity and see her for what she was. I made my peace with her before she died and I'm glad I did, but it doesn't change what happened in the past. She beat me on a daily basis. It didn't matter how slight the problem was; she would slap me, kick me, and punch me in the face, back, and stomach until I would curl up in a ball to try and protect myself. While she beat me, she screamed into my face that I was the cause of all her problems. She often said if she didn't have me she'd be better off; what in the name of God had she done to deserve me. At the beginning I asked her why she had collected me from Kilkenny, but I soon learned that if I answered her back it only made the beatings more vicious. She kicked me from one side of the room to the other. I tried to hide behind Peter or the furniture, but she always caught me by the hair and pulled me out.

Mam wasn't very happy in life and she took out her frustrations on the children—mainly me. I was frequently used as her punch bag and there were times when I believe she came close to leaving me hospitalised. She would hit me so hard I couldn't draw a breath, and she was breathless from the exertion. At the beginning I cried and tried to dodge her blows, but then I realised it only made her more hysterical, so I just stood there and let her slap me. She rarely got a reaction from me, which she hated. I could see the rage grow in her eyes, and I learned at that age she could do what she wanted to my body, but she couldn't get into my mind.

My mother and I grated on each other from the beginning. I think my stepfather never accepted me and my presence ruined their marriage. Although she loved me and wanted me in her life, on some level she knew that I caused her marital problems. She took it out on me by hitting me and beating me, although she mightn't have consciously realised why she was doing it. She kicked me around the place for no reason at all, but especially if she'd been fighting with Dad. Of course there were times when I gave her plenty of reason to lose her temper. I was wild as a child and because there was such a dreadful atmosphere at home, I often went missing for days at a time. Whatever reason I gave her to be angry, however, it didn't justify the extent of the physical abuse I received.

My stepfather gave her mental torture throughout her life and he drove her crazy. He was a very cruel man and she was petrified of him. He ruled the house with an iron fist. He had lots of rules that we had to obey or there'd be hell to pay. The television had to be switched off every night at 6 p.m. and no one was allowed to speak out loud once he went to bed. We had to whisper to each other, because if he heard any talking he would leap out of bed and give the culprit a clatter across the head. He went to bed really early every night because he got up early in the mornings to drive a digger for the Department of Posts and Telegraphs. At this stage we were still living in the one room tenement flat so it was virtually impossible to keep all of us quiet. As a consequence we were packed off to bed soon after he went in.

Mam and Dad were always screaming and fighting with each other. I never saw them kiss or saw any affection between them. There were times when they were at peace with one another, but those times were few and far between. I'm sure there were occasions when they were happy together, but I have no memories of happy times between them.

Dad called Peter and I 'the bastards'. He would say that he wasn't feeding 'her bastards'. He called Mam a whore. She cried and screamed that she was his wife—why did he marry her if he felt that way? After they finished fighting he would leave and slam the door behind him. Most days were like this as far as I recollect—the routine varied very seldom.

When people say their parents fight a lot, they usually mean they argue. When I say fight I don't always mean just arguing. Mam would throw plates at the door and chairs across the room. Dad banged around the place shouting at her, but he never hit her. He didn't need to because she was already living in fear of him. During these fights, we learned to remain as quiet as mice, because any word from us would lead to the ire changing direction, and we would be at the receiving end.

Dad would invariably storm out and Mam would shout at me to clean up the mess. She usually sat at the table crying after he left while I picked up the broken plates and brought them down to the bin. I grew up wondering what I'd done to be a bastard and if that was the reason that she was always slapping me and screaming at me.

Living in Yorke Street was like living in a prison cell. Our tenement flat never smelt clean no matter how much Mam made me scrub it. The smell of babies' nappies and sweat permeated through the bed linen, through our clothes, and into our pores. I was treated like a free maid and I spent my time after school washing what crockery survived, and looking after my younger brothers and sisters.

Mam was never allowed to have any of her friends around to visit. Dad would go mad and say they were only snooping for information and would scream if he came home and found her friends in the flat. He made only one exception to this rule; he liked a woman by the name of Connie who was friendly with Mam. She was allowed to come round and spend a fair bit of time in our flat. Connie was a lovely woman and she often stopped my mother from beating me too much. On more than one occasion she interjected while my mother hit me saying, 'Jesus, Maureen! You'll kill the child! Let her go!'

In that era, however, people generally didn't interfere in each other's lives. If people were aware of this type of violence today, they would call it child abuse, but in the fifties and sixties it was known as discipline. In those days if people saw a child being kicked around the place, they'd look away because it was considered normal, or acceptable at the very least.

. . .

About six months after I moved into Yorke Street it burned down. Peter and I were messing and we set fire to the bed by accident. We never told Mam what happened or I don't think we would have survived the beating. I brought home a kitten that I found and hid her under the bed. I took her out and played with her when no one was around. She slept in a shoebox and I fed her on milk and bread. I didn't tell anyone about the kitten because I knew that I'd have to get rid of her if Mam or Dad found out. One day Peter saw me under the bed and realised that I was hiding something.

'What have you got there?' he asked.

'Nothing; there's nothing at all,' I replied, but as I said the words the kitten gave a loud 'miaow'. I yelped and tried to cover the sound, but Peter grabbed a box of matches from beside the cooker. He put a lighting match under the bed. I jumped on top of him to try and wrestle him away from the bed, but as I did, he dropped the match, which landed on the blanket. Within seconds the bed was on fire. My sister, Margaret, was asleep in her Moses basket and we were petrified. We grabbed Margaret and ran out of the flat. The kitten ran from under the bed and followed us out. We didn't stop running until we got down the road.

That was the first time that Peter and I worked as a team. We agreed to say nothing about the fire to Mam and Dad because we knew that we would both get a beating from hell. The neighbours took us in and we stayed there until Mam came home from work. She never found out how the fire started.

.   .   .

We were rehoused to White Friar Street into a two bedroom flat, which was much nicer. We had our own bathroom and kitchen, and in that respect it was great. Mam seemed happier now that she had more space and she was able to cook in her own kitchen with a window to let the cooking smells out, instead of them constantly circulating through the living space.

I started school in White Friar Street and made lots of friends there. The school was huge. Peter went to the boys' section next door, while I went straight into baby infants. By this stage I was fed up with being a servant at home and was tired of being beaten by my mother. I got less of a beating if I said nothing and let her get on with it, but she still hit me, so I started to rebel. I just wanted to go out and play with my new friends, but I had to stay in and clean up the house the whole time.

My grandmother started coming to stay with us when we moved into the new flat. She had no time for me at all and gave me an awful life. Mam had a new baby at this stage, Michael, and I idolised him. I loved taking him out in the pram and pretending that he was my baby, but when my grandmother was around, she wouldn't let me. She slapped me a lot, and hit me over the head with annuals (the hardback childrens' comics that are published annually). When my mother saw her doing that, she went mad with her. It was okay for Mam to hit me but she wouldn't let her mother do it as well.

At my new school I hooked up with all the wild kids and we ran riot. Even at the age of five I loved going to Dunnes Stores after school and robbing lemonade and biscuits. The security guards chased my gang and we stuffed the biscuits into our mouths as we ran. I was so breathless from running that the fizz from the lemonade always made me choke, but it still tasted great. Afterwards we would run off and play in the playground or in the park. I felt freedom for the first time since I had come to Dublin during those days.

School was okay, although I had no real interest in learning. I loved getting away from home and I loved going there and meeting my friends. Those initial years at school were the last time I remember being truly carefree. I spent the next few years messing and disrupting the class, and consequently spent most of my time outside the school door.

One day when we were preparing for our First Holy Communion, the teacher discovered that I hadn't been baptised, and she sent a note home telling my mother that it was a requirement if I were to make my Communion.

I wanted no part of it, but Mam and her friend, Mrs. Collins, dragged me along to the church on the quays where I would be baptised. I was about six years old and I wore jeans and a t-shirt. My hair was short and everyone thought I was a boy. When the priest tried to pour the water over my head, I knocked the jug out of his hand and told him to 'fuck off'. My mother held me down as I tried to kick the legs off the priest. As soon as he finished baptising me, my mother released her grip and I ran out the door. I think he was sorry that he had agreed to it in the first place.

I was a real tomboy back then. I could climb any building in front of me. My mother used to say I was like a rat, because I could get through anything. I was really skinny and I'd squeeze through railings to play in derelict buildings.

There was a building site beside our flat complex and we made traps for the workmen by putting down newspapers with stones over them. We'd hear them screaming as they fell down the holes and we literally rolled around the floor laughing at them. I set traps for Peter a few times and he broke his leg once when he fell into a hole. I was sitting up in the rafters looking at him and I couldn't stop laughing. I nearly fell down I was laughing so much. He couldn't tell my mother that I had set the trap, otherwise he would have been in trouble for playing in the building site. Peter and I had a love/hate relationship throughout most of our childhood. It was hard for him too because he had been living on his own with my grandparents, and suddenly he had a ready made family. We fought like cats and dogs as children, but as we grew up we became friends.

Life continued pretty much along this vein, where I spent my days between playing and cleaning. I was happy enough for things to carry on like this, because

I was determined that Mam wouldn't get the better of me. She couldn't quell my spirit and I balanced the work and the beatings with lots of play and adventure. Then one day my stepfather decided to steal the remainder of my childhood from me.

.　.　.

I was about six years old and I was playing in my room. Mam was at work—she worked in the Shelbourne Hotel at the time—and Dad was at home minding us. My brothers and sisters were in the sitting room when he came into the room and asked me what I was doing.

I was surprised to see him as he never came near me, but he sat beside me on the bed and asked if he could watch me play. I said 'yeah' and continued with what I was doing. He lay behind me and pulled me in beside him. I felt something hard sticking uncomfortably into my back. It kept on moving, and I thought it was a toy or something in the way, and Dad was trying to move it out of the way. I tried to pull away from him, but he held on tight while his breathing got heavier in my ear. I got frightened then, and again tried to pull away, but his grip on me was too tight. I turned around and saw a fat piece of flesh against my back. It had hair around it and I was disgusted. I jerked away from him and saw him grab the fleshy thing and press it into me again. I couldn't move. After a few minutes I felt something wet against my back; he got up and walked out of the room without looking at me or saying anything.

I felt so strange and uncomfortable. I wasn't sure what had happened. He never cuddled me normally and he used to ignore me most of the time. I wanted to ask Mam about it but I was afraid that I'd done something wrong and she'd only hit me again so I didn't say anything. Instinctively I knew that it wasn't right, but I didn't know why.

Unfortunately that was only the beginning of the abuse. He came into my room quite often after that. Sometimes it was like the first time—he'd masturbate as he lay beside me. Other times he'd touch me around my private area or make me touch and masturbate him.

I didn't know how to handle it. I dreaded Mam going out when he was around. I became so angry and frustrated. Whereas before this I was just a little bit wild; now I became aggressive and angry. Things were really unbearable at home. I started spending more and more time outside of the flat. I began to worry about everything and became upset and angry at the drop of a hat. I wore myself out worrying about whether or not Dad would come into my room at night. Mam was still beating me during the day, so I suffered that ordeal in the daytime. It was a living nightmare and I didn't know how to handle it. I couldn't relate to anyone and I was stressed out and worried the whole time. When I did go to school I couldn't learn anything because I couldn't concentrate. I regularly fell asleep at the back of the class and the teacher said that I was bold and slapped me frequently.

I started going missing after that. I would avoid going home for days on end. I knew that I'd get a woeful beating when I did go back, so I avoided it as much as possible. I slept on the streets—in neighbours' sheds—anywhere really. Some of my friends would come with me because they wanted to leave their homes as well. We slept in garages and sheds, and robbed clothes and sheets off the lines to keep us warm.

During the day we robbed apples and other food. We went up to St. Stephen's Green to make money off dirty old men. There used to be a lot of men hanging around the Green and they gave us ten shillings if we felt them up. We went into the bushes with them to feel their privates and they gave us the money.

I had already been feeling Dad's privates and had started to numb myself against it, so I didn't really have a problem doing it to these old men and making money from it.

Ten shillings doesn't mean anything to people these days, but back then you could buy chips, sweets, oranges, and go to the cinema to watch cartoons for hours. I was also doing a paper round at that time for Christy Moore, a newsagent in the city. I sold papers outside St. Stephen's Green. If I didn't have enough money for food, I robbed Mary Lou's shed. Mary Lou was a dealer on Moore Street and I used to take about three or four oranges. I never robbed to sell the fruit or to make money from it—it was purely to feed myself if I was hungry.

. . .

My First Communion was coming soon and Mam took me out shopping for a dress. I was the first girl in the family, and I think she enjoyed taking me out shopping for the occasion. I liked it too, even though I normally hated anything girly. I loved having a fuss made over me and I enjoyed picking out the dress. I felt so important and grown-up. I liked the thoughts of dressing up for one day.

The morning of the Communion dawned a beautiful day. I was a bit excited about getting dressed up and I loved the idea of getting money for nothing. I went into the kitchen in my underwear to make tea for Mam, while she lay on for a bit. Dad came in and started rubbing himself against me as my younger sister, Margaret, opened the door. She saw him rubbing up against me. She just stood there in shock—it had a terrible effect on her. I pleaded with her not to say anything because I thought I'd be killed. I made her promise not to say a word and she said that she wouldn't. Both of us just blocked it out of our minds and have never spoken about it since. He never touched any of my other brothers or sisters because they were his own blood. I wasn't his daughter, so he justified the abuse because it wasn't incest.

After he abused me that morning, I felt dead inside and I knew I would never get that part of me back. I couldn't take my innocence back. Life meant nothing to me. It was a vicious hard world, and I knew it more than most. I knew about men; I knew about sex and sexuality. I was like my father's mistress. That was the thought that stayed with me as I made my First Holy Communion.

.   .   .

By the age of eight I spent most of my time on the streets trying to avoid school and home. I hated the screaming, the fights and confrontation at home. Most of all I hated my stepfather abusing me. I was terrified of him and confused by him. I always knew when he was going to abuse me because he'd be nice to me that day. I would start to shake so violently that I would drop whatever was in my hand. Mam would then clatter me across the face for breaking things. I always swore that I'd never let anyone push me around when I got older and I never did. I wanted to kill Dad when I'd see him screaming at Mam, but I never did. I was too small.

When he didn't want to abuse me, he would say to her, 'I'm not minding your fucking bastard. You'd better take her with you.'

Mam had to drag me along with her because if she left me behind someone always complained about me. The neighbours in the flats were constantly giving out about me and always had something to say.

One time Mam brought me to see a Dracula film; I had never seen it before. We were all afraid of the Mummy films but Dracula was new to me. We went to the cinema on Francis Street, which has since closed. I'll never forget how scared I was watching that film. I was petrified of Dracula and every time he appeared on the screen, the wind started to whistle. I was so convinced that he was real, and Peter helped substantiate my fears by telling me that Dracula was coming to get me.

We had a loose letterbox at home and that night there was a terrible wind that whistled through the letterbox. It must have happened before but I never noticed. But that night the wind came through the letterbox and I really thought Dracula was at the door to get me. I ran into Mam and Dad's room. Whatever way Mam was asleep, she was hanging over the edge of the bed and there was no room on her side, so I jumped in beside Dad. I thought he'd kill Dracula if he came to get me.

The only thing that got me that night, though, was Dad, and he was actually worse than Dracula. Even with Mam lying asleep beside him, he rubbed himself against me and masturbated all over me. I was so frightened I don't think I really cared. I told Mam the next morning that my pants were all sticky. He had never done it all over me like that before and I felt so sick that I vomited all morning. She turned a blind eye to it and ignored what I said. I couldn't believe that after I'd worked up the courage to tell her, she had disregarded it. I knew from that moment on that women could be just as bad as men and the only person I could rely on was me.

chapter two

When I was a little girl, I didn't like school and spent most of my time mitching or plotting how to get out of classes. On the occasions that I was present in class, I didn't pay much attention. I was too busy entertaining my friends and having a laugh. I was never able to do my homework because I always had so much housework to do, and as a consequence of this, I felt that I was stupid when I didn't know my spellings or tables. The teacher, who should have realised that there were problems at home, just perpetuated the problem by calling me bold and punishing me for not having my homework done.

I was always a bit of a joker and was a natural leader in any group situation. The girls who had no interest in learning gravitated towards me and we disrupted the class using all types of tricks. I never liked authority. I never liked people telling me what to do and I hated adhering to the school's timetable. I felt that the teachers didn't give me enough respect. I didn't change much in that regard over the years. I continued to hate anyone that represented authority and when I was working as a prostitute I fought constantly with the police.

My family didn't have much money so we didn't bring any lunch to school. Occasionally we'd bring some bread and butter but not every day. By this stage I had a few younger brothers and sisters who preoccupied my mother. Peter and I looked out for ourselves and got something to eat during the day using whatever means we could.

I preferred to spend the day making money and getting food rather than going to school. Going hungry as a child is something that you never forget as an adult. I rarely skip meals now and there's nothing I like better than meeting up with friends and going out for a meal.

Getting enough to eat during the day was one of my primary concerns as a child. I was constantly hungry and I was always thinking about food. We fed ourselves in a variety of ways. Sometimes my friends and I would do messages for old people and they'd give us bread and jam in return. Other times we sold sticks to people. We were great workers—we never stopped thinking of ways to make money. We were also earning money from men in St. Stephen's Green We turned tricks for pocket money. We spent the money just as quick by going to the pictures. I couldn't get enough of it. Even though they only changed the film once a week, I'd often go to see the same cartoon several times. I'll always remember sitting in the cinema with my friends, laughing so hard that we'd almost choke on the popcorn.

Sometimes the doctor would come into our primary school and check out the general health of all the children. The school catered for a lot of children whose families didn't have much money, and the children would be very thin or frequently tired. One time when the doctor saw me, he proclaimed, 'That child is far too thin,' and he sent a letter to our family doctor.

Dr. Doyle, the GP, then sent for my mother to come down and talk about me. He told her he had received a school report saying the authorities were worried about me because I wasn't strong and that I was too thin. My mother replied, 'But she's as strong as an ox,' which was true. I spent so much time running around outdoors that I was very strong and healthy, although I was malnourished because I didn't have enough to eat.

Dr. Doyle told her that I wasn't getting enough nourishment and he sent me to a convalescent home for a few weeks.

The first time I was sent to the convalescent home, I didn't know what to expect but I loved it because I didn't have to worry about where the next meal was coming from. The people who ran the home were very kind to me. There was never a shortage of food and it was really delicious, healthy stuff. It was the only place, in fact, where food was the priority and I could eat my fill at every mealtime. There were other children there from disadvantaged families and we played together. We had great fun playing on the swings and slides in the field. There were always cats hanging around and there were cows in the fields nearby. I always preferred animals to humans so I was delighted to see the cats when I got there.

It was the first time since my mother brought me to Dublin that I didn't have to worry about being abused, either physically or sexually, and I really relaxed and enjoyed myself. I was a withdrawn and surly child amongst adults, because of my stepfather's abuse, but I blossomed when I was with my peers. I calmed down during my stay and my previous tendencies for outbursts of violence diminished. I never said anything to the nurses about what was happening at home. I was afraid of what they would think. I felt as if I was doing something wrong and that if people found out, they'd punish me or that my mother would hit me more than ever. After spending a few weeks convalescing I'd be sent home where the cycle of abuse and lack of food would start again.

The neighbours blamed me for everything that went wrong in the flats. If someone smashed a window or robbed their milk, they came around and told my mother that it was my fault. It didn't matter what happened; even if a bicycle were stolen they blamed me to avoid the finger of suspicion being pointed at their own children. On several occasions they rang the police and told them I broke a window. The police then called round to our flat and Mam said, 'You fucking bastard! I can't go to work without you bringing the police to my door.' Anytime the police came, she kicked me around like a football once they left. I used to roll around on the floor trying to deflect some of the blows, while I tried to tell her what really happened. After a while I stopped bothering trying to explain, because she never listened or believed me anyway. She just wanted an excuse to take her anger out on me.

Whenever this happened my stepfather would stand there listening to the accusations saying, 'I'm not feeding them bastards.' So my mother didn't give us anything to eat when he was around, because she was afraid of angering him and making a bad situation worse.

I was often so sore going to bed and so weak with the hunger that I couldn't sleep. I would lie there worrying and wondering if Dad was going to come into my room. On the rare occasions that there was food at home, I would get too worried to eat and a few months later I'd end up back in a convalescent home.

. . .

I was making money from prostitution before I even heard the term. I started off making money in St. Stephen's Green as a six or seven year old girl, and progressed to working in a brothel of sorts on Benburb Street.

When I was eight years old I ran away from home again. I had often spent a night or two in someone's shed before this, but Mam always found out where I was and brought me home. If she didn't find me, I usually went home of my own accord because I was so cold. I knew that I couldn't stay in my friend's house without my mother knowing where I was, because all the mothers kept in touch with one another.

One crisp spring morning when I was mitching off school and hanging around St. Stephen's Green, one of the older girls, told me about a woman in Benburb Street who would give me food and let me stay with her. Men would come in to the house and I would only have to give them a handjob or a blowjob, which is what I was doing anyway. I was hanging around parks and street corners a lot at this stage and the girl thought I would be safer in this woman's house.

The woman's name was Cathy and her boyfriend, Paul, owned the house. Cathy took in young girls to work and she worked as a prostitute alongside them.

There was a really big room with a lovely comfortable bed and Cathy let us stay there all day watching television and eating. The men would come in and tell Cathy which one they wanted. They usually picked me, 'the one with the big eyes'. They didn't ask how old we were, but it was obvious that the oldest girl would have been around ten years of age. At eight years, I was the youngest and Cathy was the oldest at 20 years. We gave the men a handjob or a blowjob, and continued watching cartoons when we finished. The men came by the dozen and we did business with them every day; it was like a conveyer belt. Cathy handled the money. The men paid her and at the end of the day she gave us some pocket money. We made serious amounts of money, but it never lasted long.

The first time I went to Cathy's I stayed for a week. Someone told my mother where I was staying and she came to the house to bring me home. Cathy knew that I had run away from home, so she told my mother that I wasn't there. I hid under the bed when Mam came into the bedroom but I stayed as quiet as a mouse, hidden by the bedspread.

Mam didn't believe Cathy when she said she hadn't seen me, so she went down to the Bridewell Garda Station and reported me missing. Two policemen came up to the house and found me. One of them grabbed me by the legs and pulled me out from under the bed. I was roaring and kicking so the garda slapped the legs off me. He gave me an awful walloping and brought me home. The policemen said my mother was terribly worried about me, and she seemed relieved to see me when I got back.

As soon as I got the chance, however, I went straight back. Cathy never told us what to do; she sent the men in to us and we'd do whatever we wanted, but we never had full intercourse with them. I loved staying there because we made so much money. At the end of each day Cathy would bring us for a meal, or get fish and chips and we'd sit on the bed watching television; it was lovely. She'd light a fire and we would all sit up on the bed together. We'd never seen so much food in our lives. We went to the pictures nearly every day and Cathy bought sweets and cigarettes for us.

Three of us worked in Paul's house while he was at work during the day. When Cathy was out, we gave Paul blowjobs. One day Cathy came home early from shopping and caught me in bed with him. She went absolutely mad; she kicked me out and told me not to come back, but a few days later I returned. She had calmed down and let me back in to work for her. I think she realised that I wasn't to blame. It was all that I knew. She stayed with Paul for a few years after that, and they moved out to Ballybough after a year or so. When they broke up she became homeless and ended up working the streets again.

Even though we were only children and working as prostitutes, Cathy did us a favour. She showed us a lot of kindness. She fed us and bought us nice clothes, which our parents weren't able to afford. I was being abused by my stepfather and beaten by my mother, so Cathy's house was a better option for me at the time. We didn't have to go to school and we could eat as much as we wanted, so it really was a great place. Over the next few years, I was sent away to different schools because I was always mitching, but as soon as I came back I went down to Cathy's house again.

.   .   .

I am horrified now to think of children performing sexual acts, but while we were there we didn't see anything wrong with it. I would hate to think of any child being so sexually active and aware at such a young age, but back then it was part of my life. If it weren't for Cathy I would have been out on the streets starving. It's easy to accuse Cathy of using children to make a profit, but the truth is that she didn't know any better.

Cathy was brought up in industrial schools in Limerick and got thrown out when she was 16. Once she was old enough to leave the school, the nuns just threw her out without any backup or support. She had nowhere to go and had to fend for herself on the streets, so she ended up in prostitution. She knew nothing else. She was too young to sign on and was homeless; prostitution was her only means of survival. She slept in broken cars and buses until she met Paul and moved in with him. She had a very hard life and never got a break from anyone.

She feels guilty about the brothel in Benburb Street now and has her own demons to fight. She didn't understand what she was doing at the time any more than we did, because that was all that she had known from life. I became good friends with her as I got older, and when I was working on the streets she'd come and find me if she needed anything. I often brought her out for dinner and we had a lot of fun together over the years.

. . .

The only time I felt alive as a child was when I mitched from school, or I was caught robbing food and was brought to court. I loved the adrenaline rush and the thrill of the chase.

The first time I was brought to the children's court in Dublin Castle, I wasn't frightened at all for some reason. I looked upon it as a big adventure. I was about nine years old and I was robbing apples from an orchard in Harold's Cross when the police caught me. When I arrived in the courtroom, the judge had my school attendance record in front of her and she could see that I was rarely in school, so she sent me to St. Mary's Industrial School, Lakelands in Sandymount in Dublin. It was a policy of the government at the time to send the 'uncontrollable' children to reformatory schools to get an education.

Lakelands was quite a nice place. The nuns treated me very well when I was there. I had to attend classes, but it wasn't so bad. There were cows in the fields beside the school and they had dogs as well. We even had parties at Christmas time and it was just a normal routine. There was no violence and no abuse, so I was happy enough to be sent there. I was let out of Lakelands within a year but I wasn't that happy about going home.

When I got home I half expected things to have changed, but they hadn't. I was only home about a week when the novelty of my homecoming wore off and my mother started losing her temper with me again. One day as she was preparing dinner, she got a pot and hit me across the shoulder with it. Tears sprang to my eyes immediately as I ran out the door; I didn't come home for three nights.

I went straight to Cathy's where I made some money and had fun with my friends. We watched television and stuffed ourselves with food. We took care of the men that came in, but it wasn't a big deal to us. My mother came to the house once again and dragged me home, but I went back to Cathy's at every opportunity.

Every time I went home Dad started abusing me. He could barely wait until Mam had left for work; he would be in my room abusing me as she walked down the street.

When the summer holidays were over I went back to my school in White Friar Street. For a while, everything was calm and the months flew by. The novelty of being back at school with my old friends soon wore off and it wasn't long before I started mitching and hanging around the Phoenix Park. Once again the police caught up with me and brought me to court for the second time.

.　　.　　.

This time I was sentenced to spend nine months in St. Joseph's Industrial School for Girls, High Park in Drumcondra in Dublin. Although the nuns ran an infamous Magdalen laundry on the same premises, they treated me fairly well. I don't think I was equally well-behaved, however. I hated the institutionalised environment and my loss of freedom. I was very free-spirited and even though I was only a child, I wanted the freedom to get out of bed and to eat my meals when I wanted, rather than following a regime that suited other people.

One day I was disrupting a class and giving cheek to the teacher so she told me I had to stay behind and clean the classroom floor as a punishment. I decided that I wasn't going to stay because I was tired of the place. One afternoon while all the girls were upstairs doing their homework, I sneaked out.

I knew that I couldn't make it past the nuns downstairs so I got through a window upstairs. It had some bars on it—I'm not sure if it was for safety reasons or to keep us locked in, but it didn't work anyway. I was so skinny that I wriggled through the window and climbed down a gutter pipe. The window must have been about 100 feet off the ground, but I felt no fear. I only felt exhilaration with the thoughts of being free.

I hit the ground with a thud and started to run. As I turned the corner I ran straight into a nun. I was so shocked that I just stood there with my mouth gaping open. The nun said to me, 'I thought I told you young fellas not to be in here, you bold boy.'

She had mistaken me for one of the local boys. I suppose it was an easy mistake. I was such a tomboy that I had begun to look like one. My brown hair was short, my face was dirty, and I was wearing jeans and a t-shirt.

'But the others are after running off and leaving me, and I don't know my way out,' I said forlornly.

She took me to the exit gate and I hopped on a bus and went straight to Cathy's. I lasted a few days before the authorities found me and hauled me back to High Park.

That was really the beginning of my life in penal institutions. My mother couldn't control me and she admitted she had lost control to the police every time I got in trouble. I had so much anger in me towards her and my father that I didn't know how to act with people. I saw her going mad almost every day, smashing things around the house. He screamed at her daily; she wrecked the place.

Every time I was caught by the police I went berserk. It would take two or three of them to get me into the squad car, because I'd be jerking and screaming my head off. They always sent for my mother and I knew I'd be in for a beating when she got me home. She regularly hauled me out of the station by the ear, but I always tried to escape from her on the way home, because she would kill me as soon as she got me in the door. She never seemed to cool down. It didn't matter when I came home; she was always waiting to slap me.

. . .

There were weekly jumble sales in Yorke Street and every year before Christmas there was a big one in the Mansion House on Dawson Street. Mam sold fruit and vegetables at the jumble sales and swapped things with the other women. Our neighbour, Eileen Dunne, went with her and they'd barter and sell things. Mam used to give Eileen vegetables and she gave Mam ballroom dresses so she could make dresses for us. I loved going to the jumble sales because there was always something to look at. They sometimes had little puppies in cages, and I used to play with them to stop them whimpering. It was full of women who'd stand around smoking fags, gossiping, and selling:

'Do you like them puppies, love? Do you want to take one home?'

'Get your tomatoes here now—only a few left.'

There were piles of books, magazines, and toys everywhere. It was an exciting way to spend an afternoon. One time I saw a teddy bear sitting on top of a pile of games at one of the stalls. I walked over, picked him up, and kept on walking. I don't know why he caught my eye—I was never into cuddly toys, but he had a big fat belly, was black and white in colour and I loved him. I carried him with me everywhere and called him Buster.

. . .

One sunny October day I was walking along George's Street. It was one of those days when the Autumn hasn't quite come in yet. The air was warm from the sun and the leaves were just beginning to change colour. There were baskets of fruit outside a shop, so I picked up a couple of apples and started juggling them. They were big and juicy, and I was thirsty, so I threw one to my friend and bit into one. The juice dribbled down my chin and it was as sweet as I anticipated. Suddenly I heard the sound of someone running behind me; it was the shopkeeper, who had seen us through the window. I shouted a warning to my friend and we raced up the street.

Unfortunately for me there was a garda walking towards us. When he saw the man chasing us he made a grab for us, but my friend slipped out of his grasp and kept on going. No matter how much I pulled and tugged I couldn't get away from him. He brought me down to the station, where he soon discovered I was skiving off school, which was another black mark against me.

Mam collected me from the station and brought me home. She was beside herself with anger and said that she couldn't believe that I was back in court again. She went to town on me and beat me until I couldn't stand. My head was dizzy from the blows she rained on me. It was only when my brother walked in that she stopped beating me.

I stayed in all night and as the evening wore on I became more and more angry. I was hurt, both physically and emotionally, and I couldn't think straight. My little brother kept on trying to hug me, but I had to hold him at arms length because I was bruised all over. I couldn't believe that she would act that way out of the blue. Things had been okay since I came home because my stepfather had stopped interfering with me. Unfortunately Mam hadn't reached the same conclusion.

All evening long I plotted and planned my revenge. I wanted to make her pay for the years of torment and abuse. I wanted to hurt her the way she had hurt me.

That night while everyone lay sleeping, I took a bread knife from the kitchen drawer. I was blinded with fury and could only think about making Mam pay for everything she had put me through. I didn't know exactly what I was going to do, but I kept thinking that I was going to make her pay for hurting me so much. I quietly went into her bedroom and stood there holding the knife over her. She looked so peaceful in her sleep. I couldn't hurt her. Despite everything, she was my mother and I loved her. I stood looking at her, thinking about the life we had; how I wished that I could be everything that she wanted me to be. Suddenly she stirred and opened her eyes.

'Jesus, Martina!' she screamed as she pulled back in the bed. Dad woke up and saw me standing with the knife. He leapt forward and grabbed it out of my hands. I started crying.

'I wasn't going to do anything,' I sobbed. 'I was only pretending. I didn't mean anything.'

The next day I was due back in the Children's Court. Mam dressed me in a skirt and top, and brought me down to Dublin Castle. I brought Buster with me. Mam waited out in the main courtroom while I was put into a little room with some other children. One of the girls was crying, but I just held onto Buster and said nothing. After about two hours a garda came in and told me to come into the courtroom. I tuned out while the court authorities went through all the formalities. I was used to the drill and it didn't phase me. The garda who caught me on George's Street was there as was Mam. After the garda told Judge Kennedy about the apples and skiving off school, the judge asked my mother if she had anything to say.

My mother started crying in front of the judge and told her about the incident with the knife. She said that she had lost all control and was afraid that I would take a knife to her or my father again. She said that as bad as I had been in the past, she had never been afraid of me before, but now she didn't know what to do.

'I can't control her, your honour. She won't do anything for me. She won't go to school and I don't know where she is half of the time. Now I'm afraid of her. I never thought that I'd be afraid of my own daughter, but I am.'

I couldn't believe what I was hearing. I glared at Mam but she refused to look over at me. I hated her so much at that moment. Judge Kennedy said that she'd send me somewhere where they could control me, so she sentenced me to four years in St. Joseph's Industrial School in Clifden, Galway. As the garda took me out of the courtroom I turned to look at Mam but she didn't look once in my direction. She just sat there with her head in her hands.

chapter three

The next day the police put me on the Galway train. I was accompanied by a woman and a boy, who told me his name was Donal and he was nine years of age. We were afraid to chat any more in case the woman smacked us. I felt much older and wiser than Donal because I was a whole year older than him. He was also going to the school in Clifden and we travelled together, both of us afraid to admit our fears. The only thing that gave me any comfort was Buster, the teddy bear I had robbed from the sale of work a few months previously. It was only my second time on a train and this time was almost as bewildering as the first. All the other reformatory schools I had been in were based in Dublin, and I knew my friends weren't too far away. This time I didn't even know where

Clifden was. It might as well have been on the moon as far as I was concerned. I had heard whispers on the corners about children who had been sent to this school in the wilderness of Galway and the stories were too horrible to contemplate. I had a lump in my throat throughout the long journey down.

The fields and bogs whizzed by and it got dark quickly. By the time the police collected us off the train and brought us to Clifden, it was fairly late. There were a few grey, stone buildings that looked more like a prison or workhouse than a school. As I stepped out of the car, the wind seemed to howl even louder and it whipped around me, stinging my eyes. We were brought inside to the hallway where a nun met us. I was so tired I could hardly stand, but she brought us in and made us strip down to our underwear. It was so cold you could see your breath in front of your face, but I was so embarrassed at having to undress in front of Donal, that I didn't really notice. I was brought into a separate bathroom where I was scrubbed with scalding hot water. The nun gave me a nightdress to change into—a long, grey granny gown that fell to my ankles.

'Now,' she began, 'you're here for a long time and there are two ways you can do things. You can do them the right way or the wrong way. If you want to get along and not cause trouble for yourselves you'll do what you're told, when you're told. There's no point in creating trouble. And you,' she said looking at me clutching Buster, 'Give me that teddy bear! You're too old to have toys.'

She grabbed him out of my hands and told Donal to follow her towards the boys' dormitory. Another nun came out and gave me some clothes: another grey nightdress; a red pinafore dress; a navy mac to wear in the rain; a pair of black lace up shoes, and some socks and underwear. She told me to put them on the table when I got to the dormitory and indicated towards the stairs where I should lead the way.

By this time my feet were as numb as ice blocks from standing on the cold tiles. I stubbed my toe on the way up the stairs and stopped to rub it, but I got a slap from behind.

'Come on now; we don't have all night. The other children are in bed.'

The beds had lovely bright red bedspreads on them and the sheets were crispy and clean. As I climbed into bed and looked at the sleeping children around me, I just felt grateful I would be spared from my stepfather's sexual abuse for the near future. I thought that things couldn't be too bad in here if I did my time and got out quickly. I thought it might be nice to see another part of Ireland and to stay by the sea. I thought the stories I had heard must have been exaggerated; but I was sorely mistaken.

. . .

Although I was only 10 years old, I had experienced more than my fair share of violence and suffering in life. I thought I was strong and independent. I considered myself a survivor because I had put up with my mother's beatings and my father's abuse, and while it affected my disposition and made me aggressive and surly, I was able to take care of myself.

When Judge Kennedy sentenced me to four years in Clifden I didn't flinch. I had already spent a lot of time in reformatory schools, and the care in them was always better than my home environment, so I expected Clifden to be the same. I was in for a rude awakening.

The nuns in the school were a breed of their own. Some of them were the most vicious, vindictive, and inhumane people I have ever met. I don't know how they called themselves Christians and prayed to God every day, while they inflicted such horror on innocent children. One or two of the nuns were kind, but they were the exceptions to the rule.

We gave all the nuns nicknames according to their personal quirks and favourite methods of punishment. Sister Gestapo was probably the worst of them all. She couldn't pass me without slapping me across the head with her keys, or slapping me across the face. Almost all the nuns carried a leather strap they frequently used on us. If we heard them coming behind us in the corridor, we'd turn around to face them, because they were less likely to slap us on the face with it but nine times out of ten they'd slap us across the back of the head with the strap. I have often pondered upon the reasons that might have made them that way, but I never came up with a valid reason to justify any of their cruel acts.

I don't think I really felt the cold properly until I came to Clifden. The wind that came in from the Atlantic Ocean would nearly cut you in half. My face was chapped and sore for the duration of my stay there. At least when I was at home Mam or Dad would light a fire in the winter, and we'd huddle together to keep warm. Clifden was the only school where I wished myself back home, so you can imagine how difficult it was there.

At night we slept in dormitories. The dormitories were huge with high ceilings, and the wind and rain constantly beat against the windows. The room never got warm. A girl called Sally slept next to me and we soon became firm friends. We each had a rough grey blanket under the bedspread; the type that made our bare skin itch. It didn't keep the cold air out very much and we were constantly freezing. Most of the girls had chilblains and we simply had to contend with the pain, because we were never offered anything to soothe them.

Sally and I often slept together just to keep warm. We used the two blankets and wrapped up tight. It was much better than sleeping alone. If the nuns caught us we'd get a beating. One of the many rules they had was to make us sleep with our arms outside the blankets. We thought they did it just to make sure we felt the cold, but I think they were paranoid about creating lesbians. We were only innocent children, though, and making it through the night somewhat warm was our only objective. If Sally and I slept in the same bed, we made sure we got into our own separate beds before the nuns woke us in the morning. As with all their rules, they administered swift and severe punishment if they weren't obeyed. They whipped anyone they caught sharing a bed until there were welts on their legs.

·   ·   ·

The education in Clifden was abysmal. I was sent there because I was skiving off school and was uncontrollable, but in reality I wasn't sent there to get an education. I spent most of my time working. Firstly, the policy of the era was to educate through fear; secondly, most of the classes were taught through Irish, so I hadn't a chance. I had missed so much school in Dublin that I didn't even have the basics of Irish. I was lost in the classes.

Sister Peter was my teacher when I arrived in Clifden. She was blind, but it didn't stop her being savage with the stick. She always seemed to know exactly where the culprit was from the vibrations or noises; she'd lash out with her cane, always hitting her intended target. I constantly gave her reason to lash out at me. I did terrible things on her. I tied things to her habit and stuck signs on her that said, 'Kick me' or 'I'm a blind bat'. By the time one of the other teachers would notice the sign, our class would be finished and she'd have no idea who did it, so she generally took it out on all of us.

The days in the school passed by in a pattern of drudgery, beatings, and dreariness. We finished classes at about 3 p.m., then we lined up in the back yard for a roll call. After that we went in the side door to the kitchen where we were given a big bowl of inedible porridge. It was salty, lumpy, and really horrible. You could have used it as wallpaper paste it was so sticky. We had to eat every bit of it, or we'd get a lash of the cane across the back of our heads. Sugar was a treat seldom seen. We only had some milk poured over the porridge. After that we were sent into the field for playtime. It didn't matter whether it rained, hailed, or snowed. We were sent out in all weathers with just a thin mac to keep the wind and rain off. We huddled together like cattle to keep warm. It was called playtime but we didn't have anything to play with. There were no swings or toys.

The novices were sent outside to mind us. They were dressed all in white and were usually a bit kinder than the older nuns. We went into the shed if it rained, but we still froze anyway. All we had to wear was the pinafore dresses and we were cold to the bone. Even if we had been allowed to wear trousers, it wouldn't have been so bad, but our legs were freezing in the skirts. We were only sent out to 'play' when we weren't working. The rest of the time was spent in forced labour.

There was quite a little industry going on with all the free labour. The school had a farm, a bakery, and a launderette; we manned them all and laboured in them daily. My favourite job was working on the farm. They had all types of animals: cows, pigs, ducks, and chickens. Although the work was physically tough and always dirty and smelly, I didn't mind because I always preferred to spend my days talking to animals. We cleaned out the sheds and fed the animals. It also meant that we could rob the eggs. Most of the time I ate them raw but they tasted delicious because we were so hungry. I also ate the food that was meant for the animals.

During the summer they took our shoes from us and we worked barefoot. This was terrible, because our feet got cut to ribbons and if we got blood on the floor we got beaten with the cane. There was a cat on the farm called Tiger. She was always lounging around the turf shed, and I loved playing with her. She had kittens one time and I brought her milk from the farm to feed them as they got older. She got to know me and used to come to me looking for milk every time she saw me. It's funny the things that made my time there bearable.

. . .

The bakery was located beside the farm and a girl called Ann worked there. She was a few years older than us and had been in Clifden for years. We were never allowed to work in the bakery. It was probably too good for us and they knew we were so hungry we'd end up eating the bread. Sally and I became friends with Ann and we robbed eggs from the farm to give to her. She cooked them for us by putting them into a loaf of uncooked dough. That was pure heaven. The bread was so fresh it would melt in our mouths. When we bit into the soft, warm dough, the egg was gently cooked in the middle.

We always left a few eggs behind for Ann to have after we'd gone. We had to sneak in and out very carefully or we'd get a beating if we were caught inside the bakery. Some of the novices would turn a blind eye to this because they knew how hungry we were.

The worse job that I was given during my time in Clifden was weeding the nuns' graveyard. It was a nightmare. We weren't given any gloves or gardening instruments. We used our hands and pulled the weeds until our fingers bled. I stopped to suck them every now and then until I received a smack across the back of the head. We weren't allowed take a break at all or we got a cane across our back. It was bad in the summer when the nettles stung, but it was far worse in the winter when the ground was so hard that the weeds would only break off by their stems. We often ate the tops off the weeds because we were so hungry. We had to dig deep to get them out of the ground. We couldn't leave the graveyard until it was perfect—and I mean perfect in the eyes of the nuns. If we said a particular grave had been done but the supervising nun wasn't happy with it, we got the cane across the back.

They didn't need a reason to use the stick on us. Some of the nuns were worse than others, but most of them were happy to keep us in line by using the cane or by slapping us with their hand.

One day I decided I was going to get some apples because we were all starving. There was an orchard beside the graveyard and while Sister Gestapo was talking to another nun, I sneaked off. I hoped I wouldn't be noticed, because there were so many of us cleaning the graves. I ran towards the orchard, ducking behind the graves to make sure I wasn't seen.

The apples were small and green, because they hadn't ripened yet, but I didn't care. I climbed up the tree and grabbed as many apples as I could, as quickly as possible. I ate one of the apples and it made me squint from the bitter taste but it was better than nothing. I put more into my pockets, sleeves, and down my shirt before I climbed down the tree. I saw Sister Gestapo walking towards the orchard with her habit flying out behind her. She had the cane in her hand, and I didn't know what to do because she had spotted me and there was nowhere for me to run. I ran back towards the trees and climbed up one so she couldn't reach me with the cane.

She shouted up at me, 'You've got two seconds to come down out of that tree, or I'll whip you so badly you'll need a cane to walk with.'

I stayed where I was hoping she might get tired of shouting, but knowing that she wouldn't.

'Martina Keogh, if I have to climb that tree myself and drag you out, so help me God, I will.'

I looked down; her cheeks had two red spots in them and her eyes were almost bulging out of her head.

'I'll come down if you don't hit me.'

'Lord, give me patience! You'll come down this minute or I'll drag you down by the hair.'

I knew that she meant this so I slowly started to climb down. As I neared the bottom where she could reach me, she dragged me by the leg from the tree. I put my hands out to break the fall but it didn't matter. She was already hitting me across the backside with the cane before I landed. She whipped me until she was breathless and her habit was crooked. My legs started to ooze blood, but I wouldn't cry. No matter how hard the nuns tried to break my spirit, I wouldn't let them win.

· · ·

I was working in the laundry the day Donal caught his finger in one of the machines. Only the two of us were there at the time and nobody was supervising us. I was washing the clothes when I heard him scream. I turned around and saw his finger gone and blood gushing out of his hand. There was a machine with teeth wheels in it and somehow he got his finger caught in it. My stomach turned. I went outside and vomited and vomited. I was so shocked that I ran off and hid in the turf shed. I hid for hours. I kept visualising his missing finger. He was only about ten years old and had been left in a room with dangerous equipment. There was nobody watching us and I don't know what happened him after that or if he was even brought to the doctor. He was left with only half a finger.

.   .   .

There was a nursery attached to the school and we used to help mind the children. My job was to feed the babies. They were always crying with the hunger, the poor little things, and we got punished if they cried. We fed them goody—bread, milk, and sugar. That was the only nourishment they got. The older girls and nuns who looked after them full-time lined the toddlers up on the potties and left them sitting there for ages. They weren't allowed move until the nuns were sure they were finished, which could be anything up to half an hour.

If anyone ever wet the bed whilst in Clifden, they were made carry their wet sheet around the grounds until it dried. I never had that problem, thank God, but one little boy always sticks out in my mind. He was only a young child and it didn't matter how much they caned him or humiliated him; he couldn't stop wetting the bed. I'll never forget seeing that little boy begging not to be put in the field. He was terrified of the cows. He cried his heart out but it never made any difference. None of us could help him; we could only watch helplessly as he stood there screaming and crying.

．　　．　　．

Sunday was a day of rest at school in Clifden. Although the nuns failed in their Catholicism and Christianity, they acknowledged this aspect of religious life and subsequently filled our day with 'leisure' activities and prayers. The day started and ended with prayers, as did every other day, but on Sundays we had extended versions of prayer time. I hated going to Mass and being forced to pray, and I haven't attended Mass much since I finished school.

Every Sunday without fail we walked from Clifden to Letterfrack. We were lined up two by two with the nuns in front of us and behind us. We always met the boys from Letterfrack going on their walk at the same time. I knew one of them, Gerard, from home and I used to roar over to him, but the nuns would give me a clatter with the stick every time. Gerard was always very funny and he'd do things to make me laugh when I saw him. We used to laugh at the boys—they were dressed in their little short trousers, with their grey coats and hats. We found their outfits very funny because we were so used to seeing them in jeans and t-shirts.

The nuns always had sticks with them, but they were really clever about using them. They'd hide the sticks under their cloaks. We were freezing but they always had big, black cloaks on and never suffered the weather.

We walked for miles and were out for hours. We were exhausted at the end of the day and barely had the energy to stay awake for the prayer service in the evening.

. . .

I didn't spend the entire four years in Clifden. After about two years, I was sent home. I received an injury when one of the nuns pushed me into a door and when my mother found out, she somehow managed to get me home.

A group of us had been out picking blackberries in the meadow; two of us got delayed on the way back and were late returning. When we arrived at the school, one of the nuns was waiting.

She went mad and told the boy with me to pull his trousers down. When he did she beat him very badly with a cane. When I saw the beating he got I knew there was no way she was going to do the same to me. When she told me to pull my knickers down, I refused. She went to grab me and I pushed her away from me. Whatever way she fell, her habit came off and she was in a temper. She ran at me and pushed me against the door, which had glass in the top half of it. My right hand went through the door and the brass knob hit into my chest. I pulled my arm out and there was a huge piece of glass sticking out of my arm. The nun went off and left me there and Mary, who worked in the kitchen, came out to me. She removed the glass and wrapped my arm in a white cloth. They didn't bring me to the doctor or hospital to get my arm or chest examined.

My chest was extremely sore for weeks afterwards, where the knob had struck me. I was crying with the pain most evenings but nobody cared. I started getting a lump there and it was very painful to touch, but I thought that girls' breasts grew one at a time. At the same time I started vomiting; I was in the throes of developing septicemia from the injury.

One night I was crying loudly and one of the nuns came in to me. I wouldn't show her my chest because she wanted me to lift my nightdress and I wouldn't, so she got a stick and slammed it into my back. Sister Ann heard my cries and came to see what was wrong. When I told her about the pain in my chest, she brought me into the toilet so I could show it to her in private. When she saw the lump on my chest she said, 'Jesus!' and put the nightdress back on. She told me not to worry; that she'd take care of it and she put me back into bed. It seemed like I was there for hours when she took me out and brought me down to a doctor's house. He gave me some injections and I was brought to the Regional Hospital in Galway in an ambulance. I had a major operation and had a drain in my chest for weeks afterwards.

Two nuns came to visit but it was only to make sure I wasn't saying anything to the doctors. 'Did you tell them how it happened?' they asked, but of course I didn't. I knew even if I said something that no one would believe me because I was just a wild child from Dublin. After a few weeks I was sent back to St. Joseph's in Clifden where the routine of beatings and starvation started again.

It transpired later that my mother had no idea I was in hospital but she found out at a later date by accident. She started investigating the circumstances and conditions in St. Joseph's and somehow managed to get me out. I don't know how she did it, but I didn't have any idea of what was going on at the time.

One night about 5 a.m., Sister Rubberball woke me up. It was pitch dark. She gave me some new clothes—a skirt, shoes, underwear, socks, top—then brought me out to a car where there were two old men waiting. I was terrified. I didn't know what was going on, but I had to get in anyway. I didn't know where I was going. I thought they were going to bring me off and murder me. I couldn't see out of the car and I was rattling with nerves.

When I saw the first light of day I was thrilled. I could see the bogs. I recognised the way to the train station, but these men never spoke a word to me. The journey lasted about two hours, but it seemed like 20 hours to me. They brought me to the train station and put me on the train. Although I was a lot older than the child that came from Kilkenny on her own, I felt equally vulnerable. I realised I was probably going home, but I had mixed feelings about it. Mam met me off the train and whispered she was sorry as she hugged me close to her.

chapter four

Things were different when I got home. I had been away for two years and had grown up a lot during that time. There was no way Dad was going to touch me again, and he knew it. When I saw him for the first time I gave him a look that said I would kill him if he went near me. Having spent the last two years starving in Clifden, I was as skinny as ever, but at least I was free to eat whenever I pleased.

My mother had taken to ignoring me since I came home. I think she wasn't happy to have another person under her feet. Wherever I went, trouble soon followed. Not a day would go by where I wouldn't get into trouble at home. The neighbours really played up on that. There was one particular neighbour who was forever telling tales about me. If she caught me smoking she would tell my mother, who would dispense a beating. If I hit this neighbour's daughter, Mam would give me a beating. I got to the stage where I beat my neighbour's daughter for the sake of it, because I knew she'd tell on me, even if I did nothing. I had enough of trouble and enough of being beaten so I started sleeping rough again. I went around the area, found a few dogs and brought them back to the shed to sleep. I slept in cowsheds with stray dogs, because I felt very safe sleeping with them.

One time I found this beautiful dog and gave it my Dad's dinner out of the oven. When Mam found out what I'd done she screamed so loudly she almost shattered the windows. I heard her screams from the yard downstairs so I ran off and didn't come back for about two days. I went to the Oliver Bond flat complex with my friend Fran. We slept in the sheds; I robbed clothes off the line and made blankets out of them.

I robbed milk from outside shops for breakfast, but on the second day the police caught me. They brought me home, and my mother went completely berserk. The police told her what happened and told her to make sure that I stayed indoors until my court appearance. She was absolutely furious with me: firstly for giving my stepfather's dinner to the dog, and secondly for bringing the police to her house. She hated any dealings with the police and would go mad when they'd knock on the door. She told them she would keep me in line come what may and as soon as she closed the front door, the punches started to fly. She slapped me across the face and screamed that she wished she had never taken me back. I told her to 'fuck off' and that set her off completely.

She really used me as her punch bag that day and left my face a bloody mess. My nose started to bleed and my right eye closed up. I lay on the floor curled in a ball while she kicked my back and legs, and she only stopped when she had no energy left. Although I felt as if I were grown-up at this stage because I'd been through so much, I was only 12 years old. I wasn't able to protect myself against her. Despite everything I still longed for her love and approval and I couldn't believe she would hurt me so much after I'd been away for so long. Every blow that fell on me hurt much more than the beatings I received in Clifden because it was my own mother hitting me.

. .

A few days later, I was brought to court for robbing milk. I was brought in front of Judge Kennedy again, who knew me from my previous appearances. I had already spent time in a lot of the State's reformatory and industrial schools by this stage—Clifden, Lakelands and High Park. Judge Kennedy asked my mother if she could keep me under control and guarantee that I would behave myself.

My mother said she couldn't guarantee anything; I was my own person and as much as she tried, she had no control over me. The judge listened carefully and didn't say too much. She knew I had been in Clifden and I came home as wild as ever.

'I don't know if anyone can control you Martina. You will have to learn that you have to obey your parents and their rules. I'm sending you somewhere now where you'll have to obey the rules.'

She sentenced me to St. Anne's Reformatory School in Kilmacud, Dublin, for two years. St. Anne's initial remit was to cater for girls under the age of 17 who were placed in dangerous surroundings and had tendencies towards sexual immorality. It ended up, however, being just another reformatory school. If the State was so keen to keep me from sexual experiences, it should have removed me from my home when I was five years old, instead of worrying about me when I was 12.

I had been held on remand in Kilmacud lots of times when I was waiting for my court case to come up, so I was familiar with the building and the set up. There were only about 20 girls in Kilmacud and we were divided between upstairs and downstairs. Girls under 14 years of age were kept upstairs while the older girls lived on the bottom floor. I was sent up to the children's hostel because I was still only 12. There were a few girls detained with me at the time, but it was quite an intimate number.

We were supposed to work in the school as well as attend lessons, but I refused to do anything. It was part of our duties to clean the school and dormitories, but we spent most of the time chasing each other around with mops. A woman came in to teach us, but we didn't learn anything because we were too busy messing around.

The conditions in Kilmacud weren't too bad and the staff were generally very nice to me. We always got plenty to eat, but I hated being locked up; I missed hanging around the streets. The staff never touched me or hit me during my time there. The only punishment I received was having my cigarettes taken off me and being denied dessert. I never minded the latter anyway because I hated the dessert, which was always sweet rice or custard.

I had great craic winding up the nuns and teachers. I always took charge of the crowd and encouraged the other girls to play during the classes. During one knitting class, I shoved two balls of wool down my bra to make my chest look bigger. Sister Dominic realised they were missing and went crazy looking for them, but I couldn't give them back to her. She knew someone had taken them and I noticed her looking at my chest, but she didn't say anything to me.

Most of the staff were lovely but there was a nun there that hated me. We called her Hoppy because she only had half a foot and used to hop around the place. She hated me and blamed me on everything that went wrong. Whenever somebody did something wrong, she immediately blamed me and claimed to have witnessed me doing it, even when I was innocent. She always said she saw me doing things 'with her own two eyes,' even when she clearly hadn't. One day one of the girls put a chair through the window during a row. Hoppy came down and told the other nun that she saw me doing it. I told her I didn't do it but she kept on insisting I did. She said she had watched me 'with her own two eyes.' I could feel the rage building up inside me and I said, 'Hold on a minute!' I picked up a chair and flung it through the other window.

'Now you saw me do it with your own two eyes.'

It wasn't any wonder that she didn't like me, though. We did terrible things to her. One day we tied her up, threw her into a bath of cold water and left her there. I think she was afraid of us after that because we weren't punished for it, so maybe she didn't tell the others what happened.

Another thing I hated about being in Kilmacud was that we had to go to Mass every day. We would get up at 6 a.m. every day and go to 7 a.m. Mass before classes. I disrupted Mass all the time. I could never sit still and I didn't think I should have to attend. I used to stick pins into the girls in front of me so they'd roar out load and everybody would laugh. Other times I made faces at people or flicked stones at them. I was a nightmare.

One day I discovered that the key to the sacristy also opened the exit door. I told my friend Helen about my plan and she said she'd escape with me. I never went to confession for the nuns, but when I discovered the key I went to the priest looking for confession.

'Well my child. Are you here for confession?'

'It doesn't matter. Leave it, I don't want it,' I said as I slipped the key into my pocket.

Helen was waiting for me outside so I gave her the key and the two of us escaped. We ran down the avenue and hopped on the first bus into town. We decided to get our friend, Katie, out of High Park so we could go around town together. When we arrived at High Park, we told the nuns we were Katie's sisters and we needed to talk to her. We had planned on running into town once she came out. We thought we were so clever. They gave us biscuits and sandwiches while they got Katie.

Unfortunately the nuns realised who we were, and while we were munching the sandwiches they called the police. I couldn't believe it when I saw two policemen walk through the door. I knew immediately we'd been rumbled and I made a dash for the door, but one of the policemen caught me by the arm and dragged me into the squad car.

When they brought us back to Kilmacud, the nuns locked me in the detention room all night. It was like a cell; it was just a wooden bed with a toilet. They said I was the ringleader and the cause of all the trouble, so they locked me away. I'm not sure how they punished Helen, but she wasn't locked up like I was.

When they let me out, I was so angry I smashed every plate I could get my hands on. I was asked to clean the kitchen but I was so annoyed and upset that I wrecked the place. I was never put on kitchen cleaning duties after that.

After I was locked up in the detention room I got really depressed and fed up. Everywhere I went I got into trouble, and I seemed to be punished more than the 'crime' deserved. One day I couldn't stand being there any more. I was sweeping the corridor floor when I decided I had enough of being confined. I told one of the nuns that I'd break all the windows in the place if she didn't open the gates and let me out. I had a brush in my hands and I was going to smash every one of them. She knew I was capable of it, even though I was only 13, so she had no choice.

'I'm going to get the key to let you out, Martina,' she said. 'Wait here and don't do anything.'

She came back with a senior member of staff who said, 'Now, Martina, there's no need for that. What's wrong with you?'

'Open the fucking gate now or I'll smash all the statues as well!' I screamed as I raised the brush over my head and aimed it at a large statue of Mary and Jesus.

'Okay, Martina,' the supervisor said. 'You're free to go.'

As soon as they opened the gate, I ran off and hid in the Phoenix Park until the police caught up with me.

When I was caught this time, I was put on remand in a city centre convent. When arrested I was wearing trousers, but trousers were against the rules. There was a doddery old nun on duty and she told me I should be wearing a skirt; I told her I lived just around the corner and I'd run to my house to pick up a skirt. The poor old nun let me go and I ran off and didn't come back. The police caught me shortly afterwards and brought me back to the convent. I had three months to go until my fourteenth birthday and I worked in the laundry until that time. It was slave labour. We washed clothes morning, noon, and night and never got any money for it. I hated it.

.   .   .

One sunny day in July, I turned 14. I had done my time in the laundry so I was free to go. I went home, but Mam and I still had an uneasy relationship, although it was better than it used to be. She stopped beating me and I stopped winding her up. My relationship with my stepfather continued to be non-existent.

I spent a lot of time on the streets. I still went home every now and again. I made money by giving handjobs to men in the Phoenix Park. While I was waiting for business, I played in the playground. A steady stream of men went to the playground looking to do business. There were already some girls working there and we always made enough money to eat and to get through the day. In one sense it was a carefree existence.

We hung around the Rainbow Café in town when we weren't doing anything else. We would get chips and spend hours eating them; just watching people coming and going. Whenever the police would come in looking for people, we'd run and hide in the ladies, because they wouldn't search in there. We were always afraid we'd be arrested and sent to an industrial school for skiving off.

One night my friend, Sharon, and I were standing outside the Rainbow Café when we met this guy called Charlie. He had a big dog with him, which, of course, got my attention straight away. We started talking to him and told him we were just hanging around the streets and living away from home. He was really nice and said we could stay in his place anytime; there was no problem. He was probably in his thirties or forties at the time. He was with a quiet fellow called Eddie.

We went back to Charlie's thinking we would hang around listening to records, but when we got back, it was a completely different story. As soon as we got in the door, the men became very aggressive in their manner and grunted when we asked them a question. Charlie started talking on the phone, while Eddie sat down and stared at us. We sat on the couch, realising that we shouldn't be there, but not knowing what to do. I was petting the dog the whole time wondering if we could escape, but Eddie was sitting in the way of the door, and I knew that I might make it out but Sharon wouldn't. The tension was awful. After about 30 minutes three more men came in. Charlie told us to go into the bedroom, so Sharon and I huddled together on the bed.

Before we even had a chance to talk, one of the men came in and dragged Sharon away from me. She tried to jump up and pull away from him but he started beating her. He pulled off her clothes, grabbed her breasts and kept on smacking her on the head until she was semi-conscious. While he was doing that another man came in and I switched my mind off. I didn't put up a fight because I knew what would happen. The men came in one after another and raped both of us again and again.

It was a nightmare situation; we were trapped and held like animals. I had never had penetrative sex before and I bled nonstop but it didn't make any difference to those bastards. I was so bruised and tender; I thought they would murder us when they had finished. They kept us in that bedroom for about two days and every morning and evening they left sandwiches and lemonade in the room for us. At night, four or five men would arrive and rape us. It didn't matter how sore or bruised we were.

We were lucky to escape. Charlie went out one day and forgot to lock us in the bedroom. Sharon opened the bedroom door and we escaped through the kitchen window. We had to drop two storeys to get away, but we were so scared and sore that we didn't care. We clambered down by clinging onto a drainpipe. That was a very painful learning experience and after that I was careful not to go back to anyone's place, no matter how nice they seemed.

I started mixing with a few women who worked on the streets, although I wasn't doing it full-time. One day I was in St. Stephen's Green with them when a fight broke out. One of the women was teasing another girl, so the girl battered her. The woman who received the beating went off with minor injuries and the girl started telling us about the fight. In the middle of this the police arrived and arrested the whole lot of us for being disorderly.

They put us on remand in Mountjoy Jail. I told them I was 17 and spent a week in a cell on my own. I thought it was preferable to be in Mountjoy than any of the homes that were run by the nuns. My mother found out that I was in prison and told them I was only 14, so they let me out under her supervision. I told her why I had been arrested and for once she believed me.

One night I was in town with Mam when we had a row. She chased me as far as Aungier Street, threatening to kill me. There was a car showroom there full of brand new cars—they were magnificent looking. I stopped outside the showroom and said to Mam that if she took one step closer to me, I'd put a brick through the window. She went to grab me so I picked up a brick, threw it in the window and ran off. The alarm started to go off as I ran, so I looked around and saw that one of the cars was destroyed.

I spent the next few nights on the streets hiding from my mother and the police but they caught me after a few days. For once it wasn't my mother who told them what I had done, but a woman who knew me had witnessed the whole thing. The police brought me to court to decide where I should go. The judge sent me back to Kilmacud for a year, but this time I was downstairs with the older women. One girl in particular, Judy, really took me under her wing and looked after me. She had spent most of her childhood in industrial schools. We clicked immediately and became great friends.

Although I knew about sex, I was innocent in lots of ways. I remember when one of the girls was leaving Kilmacud I asked her where she was going. She said she had to leave because she had the pox. When one of the nuns asked where Mary was, I told her what she had said and the nun gave me a strange look. I thought Mary was talking about the chicken pox; I didn't realise she had syphilis until someone explained it to me later.

I learned all about prostitution from the older girls in Kilmacud. A few of them had been on the game before they were brought to Kilmacud and they told me it was a great way to make money. Most of the girls had no family. There were reared in these schools and then dumped out on the streets when they hit 16. Most of the time they would meet guys on the street and get chatting to them. These guys would pick them up and be nice to them. The girls had never received any kindness or affection while they were in the schools and fell in love with these men. They didn't realise the men were pimps. The pimps preyed on vulnerable girls who had nobody to turn to. They always picked on the girls that didn't have a big family. Of course, the girls would be so fascinated and mad about them that they'd work all the hours God sent, and give their pimps every penny. If the girls started to slacken at all, the violence would start.

Of course I only heard about the good side of prostitution when I was in Kilmacud. The girls told me about the great money and the freedom of working their own hours. The girls had been working on the street before they were locked up and were planning on going straight back as soon as they got out. They told me how much money they made on the streets and how their men looked after them. I knew what I would do when I left Kilmacud. It's what

I had been doing my whole life, but I hadn't made much money out of it. This time would be different. I spent about a year in Kilmacud and didn't bother going home when I got out.

chapter five

As far as I was concerned I was now finished with my family—they weren't my family any more. I was on my own in the world and it was time to start looking out for myself. I started sleeping rough.

One day when I was in St. Stephen's Green, I bumped into Judy, one of the girls I befriended in Kilmacud. I told her that I was hanging around, making some money in the Phoenix Park and in the Green, and sleeping in sheds as I had done throughout most of my childhood.

Judy was working on the streets as a prostitute. She told me she was making a fair bit of money—certainly a great deal more than I was. She lived in a bed and breakfast in Rathmines and invited me to come and stay with her. That night I moved into the B&B. It was great. I loved having the freedom to come and go as I pleased without having to worry about being molested. After a couple of days I needed to start earning proper money, so I asked Judy to take me to the red light district and show me what to do.

The streets of Dublin are divided quite neatly when it comes to prostitution and everyone stays on their own patch. There are invisible boundaries between the areas, and if a prostitute strays off her usual beat, that's when problems occur between the women and the pimps. Judy brought me to Burlington Road where she worked and I came in as her friend, so there was no problem. Sometimes the women are very possessive about their areas, but they welcomed me.

I felt physically sick that night. I realised I was making a life-changing decision, and whatever I had done in the past to survive, this was taking it one step further. When I was a child getting money off men, I thought it was just a transient thing and I wouldn't be doing it forever. When I walked down Burlington Road for the first time as a prostitute, however, I knew there was no turning back. This scared me.

We arrived on Burlington Road at about 8 p.m. It was a lovely evening. The air was warm and hazy; there were a few clouds drifting slowly along the skyline. Judy introduced me to one or two of the women that were standing around. We smoked a few cigarettes and chatted. I was the youngest and the girls on the beat seemed much older and wiser than me, but in reality most of them were probably only about 19 or 20. They were friendly and welcoming. After a few minutes, a man approached us and asked if we were doing business. Judy said we were and asked me to get in the back of the car while she sat in the front. She gave him a handjob while I watched. I didn't feel anything while I watched them; I was desensitised to sex by this stage. The punter must have gotten an extra thrill out of it because he gave her more money for me being there. It felt a little surreal to sit there watching this happening, but it was over really quickly—within 10 minutes—and we had made so much money.

When we got out Judy gave me some money for the job along with two golden rules. She told me never to do anything without getting the money upfront and always use a condom. She said that men often offered extra money if the girls would go without, but not to be tempted. I never forgot the rules and have passed them to any new girl that I met along the way. It was illegal to buy condoms in the Republic back then, so one of the girls, Deirdre from Belfast, always bought a few kilos of Durex for £14. Every time she went home we gave her money and she came back laden with condoms. In all my years of working as a prostitute, I never went without condoms, no matter how much money was offered. It simply wasn't worth it, because if I didn't have my health I wouldn't be able to work. Consequently I never got a sexually transmitted disease or any infection. None of the women got any diseases because they were so careful. I was talking to a health professional some years later and he commented that prostitutes rarely get STDs because they are generally fanatical about their sexual health.

I learned a lot from the girls on the beat in my first few weeks. After about two weeks I got my period and I told Judy I couldn't work, but she told me that all the women cut up sponges and put them inside them, so it meant that we were able to work any time of the month.

I had a very rough start in prostitution. It wasn't as if I thought it was an easy way to make money, but I wasn't ready for how tough it would be. There were all types of people being abusive towards us; there were drunken men who roared at us from across the road; cars slowed down as if to look for business and when we walked over to them they drove off with their tyres screeching. As the night wore on, men would come over to us and stand there talking as if they were trying to chat us up. It took me a while to figure out that these men were curious about prostitutes, but not curious enough to have sex. They just got in the way and wasted our time.

As I observed the various aspects of the night, I didn't say anything to Judy about what I was thinking, but I just looked at her and thought, 'Jesus, is this what my life is all about?' It was very sad and lonely because it was dark and dull; the cars were pulling up bumper to bumper. There was no end of men looking for women, but I backed off most of the time and let the other women take the jobs. I literally felt sick to my stomach and I was overwhelmed by everything.

When I decided to take a job for the first time, one of the girls went with me in the car. She negotiated the money and sat with me. He just wanted a handjob, so it wasn't too bad. In prostitution someone will always go with you for the first time; after that you're on your own. The punter was a nice guy and he knew it was my first time, which excited him even more. It was over very quickly.

There was a set price for everything, and you had to go with that price or the other women would kill you. You could charge more than the going rate if you wanted, but you could never go under it. It was £10 for intercourse (but I always got £15 for it) and £7 for a handjob. It was a very good wage for 10 minutes work. That was almost 20 years ago, so it went a long way.

I had never really stood on the streets soliciting work before. In Cathy's, the men were always brought to me. In St. Stephen's Green, the men approached us while we were playing; we never stood around looking for them. On some level I knew I was in control of my body and my mind, but I didn't have control over my life. I didn't know what else I could do to make money. I had never really attended school so I didn't have a good education, although I could read and write. I subsequently educated myself by watching the news, and reading papers and books. From the night I started working as a prostitute I stopped living and merely existed.

On my second night working on Burlington Road, a car pulled up and Judy went over to talk to the driver. She came back to me and asked if I wanted to do this particular punter on my own, so I said I would. I got into the car and he didn't say a word. He drove up a lane and pulled in. He then started punching me and slapping me as he raped me. I couldn't believe what was happening. I screamed and fought back, but he overpowered me easily. As he assaulted me, I kept wondering why Judy had done this. When he finished raping me he drove back to Burlington Road, and told me to keep my mouth shut about the attack. He said that he was a garda and he'd have me arrested if I said anything to anyone. I was shaking with the fright and just sobbed in agreement. He kicked me out of the car when we pulled up and I fell onto the street. I lay there groaning and weeping.

Judy came over to me and said that she was so sorry for what he did. She didn't have a choice but to let me go with him, because he would have raped both of us and then arrested us if I didn't go. Apparently he got his kicks this way; he did this to all the new girls. None of the women ever said or did anything about it. They were all terrified of him—he was a savage bastard.

I had been attacked before and I had been raped before, but this attack caught me off guard because Judy had specially asked me to take this punter. I thought she was vetting the clients for me and I had let my guard down. I understood that Judy didn't have a choice, so I didn't hold it against her or fall out with her over it. I didn't do anyone else that night, but I never thought about not going back the following night. I suppose I got a proper introduction into the profession that way. I knew my life was fucked and there was no turning back. Once you spend a few nights working as a prostitute, you see all elements of humanity, and there is more bad out there than good. It's not easy to go back to the way you were before; the experience haunts you forever.

I was aware that somewhere along the line I could be murdered and nobody would know about it because nobody knew what I was doing. I had such a habit of disappearing for weeks on end that no one would have missed me. With all these things in mind, I started going to Burlington Road every night and that became my life. I suppose you could say that I settled into life as a prostitute. I was living in the B&B with Judy and making my own money so things were going fine. I worked from 11 p.m. or 12 a.m. until 3 a.m. I only worked four nights a week, so I had a lot of free time. When we finished work every night, we'd go for a meal to Gigs restaurant on Richmond Street. That was part of the whole night; we'd sit down together, drink wine and wind down after an adrenaline filled night. A colourful group of people gathered there every night and we had great fun. I often had dinner with John Traynor, the criminal known as 'the Coach', and he always had great admiration for the women on the streets. He liked strong women and was never abusive towards us at all. All types of gangsters, loners, and insomniacs gathered there into the small hours of the morning. I was enjoying myself for the first time in years.

.   .   .

A chance meeting with a Communist changed my life. One day I was walking along O'Connell Street when I saw a march and started walking along with the protesters out of curiousity. I started talking to a guy participating in the march. His name was Noel and he was a member of the Communist Party. He was so bitter and cynical that he fascinated me. I could identify with him because of his cynicism and the two of us got together. I started staying at his flat and I ended up getting pregnant by him. Although I was only 16, I didn't mind getting pregnant. I knew I had enough experience in life to be a mother and I'd be able to cope with a baby. Everything was going fine between Noel and I at the beginning, but one day I came in and found him in bed with a friend of mine, so I left him immediately.

It didn't really bother me when I found him with my friend, because I wasn't in love with him. I was having sex with him because it was the only way I could show affection. I was still working as a prostitute, but it didn't interfere in my relationship. I was able to separate my professional sex life from my private sex life. I enjoyed sex with my boyfriend, but I switched off when I was with a punter. I didn't care how ugly they were; once they were clean I'd go with them.

There was no way I was going to stay with Noel once I knew he was messing around with someone else. I went back to Judy's flat, because I'd nowhere to go. We were great friends and it was never a problem living and working together. After a month or two, I decided to get a day job as well. I got a job in Kennedy's bakery. It was nice work, although the money wasn't great compared to what I'd earn on the streets. When I was about six and a half months pregnant I moved to a biscuit factory, where I was earning more money. My pregnancy was going well, except that I didn't put on any weight at all. I was vomiting a lot and I didn't eat much. No one could tell I was pregnant by looking at me, and I didn't tell many people.

I never had any problems getting business. Punters usually didn't realise I was carrying a baby, because I was so small. They never knew I was pregnant in the factory either. I used to stand on my feet all day and was exhausted by the evening. When I had the baby, no one at the factory could believe it, because I had spent eight hours on my feet every day and never complained.

.   .   .

Judy also had a child at this point, Seán, but he didn't live with us. He was in a children's home on the Navan Road. One night Judy told me the nuns were going to get him adopted if she didn't find anyone to take him. I told her that my mother would take Seán—she loved children and was very good to them. I was the only one she physically abused. I saw that she was good to my brothers and sisters so I told Judy that she would take her child, but I made Judy swear not to tell my mother I was pregnant. Mam hadn't a clue.

Judy and I called out to my mother and filled her in on the situation. She was always taking in kids and was delighted to take Seán. She started visiting him in the children's home and built up a good relationship with the nuns that were taking care of him. They were delighted he was being fostered somewhere that Judy could maintain regular contact with him. The three of us went out to collect him, and when we got there the nun asked Mam how she was going to look after Seán, seeing that I was pregnant. Mam replied, 'She's not pregnant.'

'I am not,' I said.

Whatever way I was standing, the nun could see that I was. She brought me outside and asked when I was due. She said she wouldn't stop Mam from taking Seán because of it, but she just wanted to know when I was due. I kept denying it at first, but then I said, 'I don't know.'

'Well,' she said, 'you're going to have your baby in ten days or less.'

When we got outside Mam asked me to tell her the truth about my pregnancy. I admitted it and she asked me to move back in with her. She said she'd help me and look after the baby for me while I worked. She didn't know I had been working as a prostitute at night; she only knew I was working in the factory during the day. I moved back into my mother's house and things were better between us than they had been in years.

About a week before my daughter was born, I gave up working on the streets. I didn't want that life anymore, and I was earning a wage during the day so I wasn't desperate for money.

As the nun had predicted, I did go into labour within ten days. In October 1970 when I was at home on my own cleaning the house, I started getting pains in my stomach. I wasn't sure if it was labour or not, so when Mam came back I told her what my symptoms were. She told me I had to wait until the pain moved to my back. The pain never moved but at about 5 p.m.

I got an ambulance into the Rotunda Maternity Hospital in the city centre.

I went in on my own, because they didn't let anyone into the labour ward in those days. Mam was looking after the kids at home so she couldn't leave them anyway. My friends and family rang the hospital every half hour to see if I had the baby yet. It got to the point where one of the nurses told them that I had a boy, just to get them to stop ringing. But I had a baby girl the next morning at 11.10 a.m. and I called her Patricia. I loved her immediately.

The labour wasn't too bad. I felt as if I had no right to complain because I wasn't married. I had gotten myself into this situation and it was up to me to deal with it. After the baby was born I had a bath and was brought down to the ward. I was mesmerised by the baby and I kept changing her clothes as if she were a doll. The nurses eventually told me to stop changing her so much. She was so tiny I used to bathe her in a bowl. I swore from the day she entered this world that no man would ever abuse her. I would kill them stone dead if anyone ever touched her. I wouldn't care if I ended up doing life in Mountjoy for it. I kept my promise to her, though, and she is a lovely grown woman now with children of her own.

While I was in the Rotunda, my stepfather started his usual act of trying to control the situation. He told Mam that I couldn't go home with the baby—I wasn't welcome there. The next day he changed his mind and said it was okay for us to go home. I didn't know what would happen. I knew they wouldn't let me out of the hospital with nowhere to go and I was terrified they would take the baby from me. I was in bits. Eventually Mam put her foot down and insisted I went home and she'd look after Patricia.

I wasn't scared about being a mother because I was very capable. I was only 17 but I had experienced many things in life and was able to handle the responsibility of rearing a child. Instinct kicked in and it felt like the most natural thing in the world to be a mother. After everything I had been through I was very strong, but I was also very anxious about bringing her into the house where my stepfather was.

Although their marriage had more or less ended, Mam and Dad still shared the same flat. I think deep down Mam knew he had abused me, but at the time she wouldn't face the truth. I insisted Patricia was never in the house on her own with him. She agreed and made sure somebody was always with Patricia when he was around.

I felt very lucky to have my daughter. She was such an easy child to mind and I really idolised her. Mam and my sister, Margaret, looked after her for me and they spoiled her with love and affection. The only thing I found very hard was getting up in the night to feed her. I was like a zombie for the first two months but gradually I got used to the night-time feeding. I was in work at 7 a.m. every day in the factory and I'll never forget how tired I was every morning.

The house was fairly crammed with people by now. There were two bedrooms but Dad stayed in one on his own. The rest of us shared the other bedroom. The baby slept with me on the bottom bunk; my sister Margaret slept with Judy's baby, Seán, in the top bunk; Mam slept in the double bed with my other siblings, Thomas, Sinéad and Gabrielle.

A few weeks after having Patricia, management at the factory called me into the office and said they'd heard I'd had a baby. They asked me if I was married and I said that I wasn't, so they told me they had to let me go. They were sorry but there was nothing they could do. I went back on the streets where I was my own boss and didn't have to answer to anyone .

.   .   .

I lived at home for the next few years. It worked out fine because Mam really idolised Patricia even though she never really got on with me. I had the freedom to go out and work at night, and I was with Patricia during the day, though Mam still treated me as a servant in the house. I did all the cooking and cleaning, but at the same time didn't need childcare so it worked to my benefit.

I always felt an awful sense of dread whenever my stepfather would pick Patricia up and I'd just grab her off him. I was terrified of him with her, especially as she got older. I started worrying about her more and more in case he'd try to go near her, so when Patricia was about three and a half we moved into a flat in Rathmines. I liked that area and I worked nearby. It was great being totally independent again.

At this point I decided to get out of prostitution once again. I got a job in a private clinic on the south side of the city, which dealt with arthritis and things like that. I worked as an assistant; that involved looking after the wards and giving out the teas and dinners. I loved mixing with people and I liked being off the streets. One day a priest was chatting to one of the women who worked in the kitchen. He knew me from the streets; he worked with some of the women in prostitution, and he told her that I was a prostitute. She told the management what I had worked as, so they fired me. The priest in question apologised to me later and told me he didn't mean for it to come out, but it was too late by then.

Once more I believed I had no option other than going back to prostitution. When I got sacked I felt as if there was no point in trying to get out of prostitution. A lot of women tried to leave it, but the streets haunted them. They couldn't escape their former life; there was such a stigma attached to the sex industry, which still exists. I realised soon after I got fired that I had to acknowledge what I was, otherwise it would eat me up. I couldn't be ashamed of the fact that I was a prostitute, or else it meant that

I would have been ashamed of myself, and I wasn't. I was making an honest living; I wasn't hurting anyone. From that moment on, I always told people what I worked as and I held my head high. If someone couldn't handle my job or they treated me badly because of it, I realised it reflected on them and their issues, not on me. I realised when I got fired that time, the only place where I had control over my job and finances was on the street, so I went back to prostitution soon after leaving the clinic.

chapter six

I soon got back into the swing of things on the streets, and although I wasn't living at home anymore, my mother still took care of Patricia for me, which meant I had a terrific amount of freedom. We were getting on very well together now that I wasn't living at home and we had a bit of distance between us. I was also able to identify with her since becoming a mother and I understood for the first time ever a love that a mother has for a child. I knew despite everything she had put me through, she loved me with a mother's passion, even though she couldn't always show it.

Sometimes I think I inherited that trait from her. I don't really have much time for people and I rarely show affection to my friends. I've always been affectionate with my daughter and her children, but not with anyone else. I always held a certain amount of myself back from my boyfriends over the years.

Although there aren't many things in my life that I'm proud of, I've always been incredibly proud of my daughter, Patricia. When she was born I swore I would kill any man that hurt her. I thank God I managed to protect her and spare her from an upbringing like mine.

She was a beautiful baby and my mother doted on her. She was the first grandchild and Mam gave her everything. My sister, Sinéad, was only eight when she was born, so they were very close. Judy's son, Seán, also lived in the house and he was only a year older than Patricia, and they were great friends.

I wasn't living in Rathmines that long when I found out that I was pregnant again. It was a similar situation to the first time, where I got pregnant by a boyfriend that I wasn't in love with; I knew we had no future together. Patricia was about three and a half and I knew I wouldn't be able to cope with another child. I was devastated. One of the women who worked with me on the streets, Michelle, offered to do an abortion when she saw the state I was in. She told me she had done lots of abortions and they always worked. I don't agree with abortion generally, but if the person is less than three months pregnant I think it's okay. Sometimes it's more cruel to bring a child into the world when the mother can't look after it properly. I knew having another child wasn't right for me.

Michelle brought me over to her flat one evening where she said she'd perform the abortion. She told me to get into a bath because it would make it less painful. I brought a bottle of vodka with me so I could obliterate any pain—either emotional or physical. When I arrived Michelle had everything ready to go.

I started drinking vodka very quickly because I wanted to be as drunk as possible. I didn't want to know what was going on and I didn't want to feel any pain. Michelle poured herself a vodka and was about to take a drink until I said to her, 'Hold on Michelle. You can get drunk with me when you've finished. Until then, you'd better stay sober.'

So she remained sober while I tried to drink myself into oblivion. I was so tense and nervous, however, that it didn't really work.

I'll always remember sitting on the edge of the bath swigging out of the bottle of vodka while Michelle poured gin into the bath. I got hysterical with nerves and I asked her if she was sure it would be okay. I didn't want to damage the baby if the abortion didn't work. I thought it was just an old wives tale that you should take a gin bath if you wanted to abort a pregnancy. Michelle assured me she had done this many times before and it had always worked; I lay in the bath for about 40 minutes keeping the temperature as hot as I could bear. I drank three glasses of vodka and tonic while I bathed and tried to read a magazine but ended up just looking at the pictures. I thought about what I was doing. I knew I was making the right decision because I wouldn't be able to bring up two children on my own. When I was done, I went into the sitting room where Michelle had a knitting needle and towels. She put the knitting needle inside me and moved it around for a few minutes. I was biting on my hand trying not to cry out with the pain; it was a horrible sensation. When she finished I was just glad that it was over and I felt relieved. We spent the rest of the night finishing the remaining vodka and gin. I bled a little after the procedure, so I thought it had worked but I couldn't be sure.

I went back to work a few nights later and felt happy about the way the abortion had gone. I was able to work and I assumed the pregnancy was terminated, because I didn't feel any symptoms anymore. A few weeks later I woke with an almighty pain in my stomach. The sheets were soaked with blood and I was haemorrhaging badly. I felt dreadful; I was lightheaded, dizzy, and I vomited all over the place because of the intense pain in my stomach. I got an ambulance into the Coombe Hospital, where I spent the following three months. They tried to save the baby, but it was too late. I couldn't tell them what I had tried to do, and I decided at that point if they saved the baby, then it was meant to be. I'd do my best to raise it properly. Despite three months of monitoring and care, the baby didn't make it. I also got blood poisoning and nearly died.

When I started to feel better, a priest came around to my bed and asked if I wanted confession, so I said, 'Yes', just to be polite. I went to the chapel with him, where he proceeded with the confession. Out of the blue he asked me if I was married. When I responded in the negative, he asked if I had any kids. When I told him I had a daughter, he asked if I was sorry.

'Of course I'm not sorry I have her,' I replied somewhat surprised.

'Well, I can't give you confession if you're not sorry.'

'Fuck off so and stick your confession up your arse,' I said as I hobbled out of the room.

I was never going to apologise for having my daughter because she was my pride and joy. I asked a friend of mine, Fr. O'Sullivan, to give me confession, and he came to the hospital and heard me confess.

. . .

When Patricia was old enough I sent her to a boarding school in Dun Laoghaire where she stayed five nights a week. Every Wednesday afternoon I visited her and made sure that she was settled and happy. She loved school because there was a lovely atmosphere in the place. There weren't many in her class and the education was very good.

When she was seven I got a corporation flat in the north inner city. I had put my name down a few years earlier to keep my mother happy, because she kept telling me to settle somewhere for the child's sake. I loved the freedom of moving around from flat to flat but I reluctantly accepted that she was right about the need for stability. Before I moved to the inner city, no one ever knew where I was. I could go missing for weeks at a time and no one would know where I would be. That was just the way I liked it.

The next few years were peaceful and fruitful and I settled into life as a mother. I was making lots of money on the streets and living well. I saw Patricia frequently and I was confident she was getting great care in school. My mother took care of her when I worked nights at weekends.

Then my mother died. I was devastated. Although she had beaten me badly over the years and treated me like a free servant, we had finally made our peace. She was still my mother and I always loved her. When my stepfather died a few years later, however, I felt nothing at all.

After the initial shock of losing Mam, I realised life goes on, as it always does, and I went back to work. I got a babysitter for Patricia when I worked on weekend nights, but otherwise our routine stayed the same. She stayed in boarding school and came home at the weekends. A few years later the school lost funding from the government and closed down. By this stage Patricia was 11 and old enough for secondary school so I sent her straight to Beaumount Secondary School after the summer holidays.

At the same time I had heard about a vacant house beside Mount Street and decided to start working indoors to get away from the streets. Things were getting more dangerous than ever and I was constantly on the watch for any perilous pimps or punters. I set up a massage parlour and I arranged for some women to come and work there. I got a percentage off them for using the house. Things were going well for a few months and I was making good money. It transpired that it wasn't that much safer than the streets, because the punters still beat us and raped us occasionally, but we were out of the pimp's sight. One night the police raided it and the *Sunday World* exposed it, so I had to close it down. One disadvantage to working as a prostitute is that you can't make any long-term plans; there are always surprises along the way.

The social workers saw the article and realised I was on my own with Patricia since my mother died so they took her from me and put her into High Park. They tried to say I was an unfit mother because I was working in a massage parlour. I was going crazy thinking about her in a reformatory school; I hated the thoughts of her there. Patricia was much softer than I was because she hadn't been exposed to the horrible side of life. She was only about 11 and I couldn't bear to think of her in there. I went to a solicitor called Garrett Sheehan and he took my case. We got Patricia back fairly quickly because they couldn't prove I was an unfit mother simply because of where I worked. I didn't bother working indoors again after that incident.

Around the same time, someone told Patricia I worked as a prostitute. I didn't really mind that she knew because I had planned on telling her some day anyway. When she asked me about it I told her it was true. I didn't see any point in denying it, because I liked having an open and honest relationship with her. She didn't get upset but she worried about me after that when I went out to work.

I tried to shield her from the violent side of prostitution, but sometimes it spilled over into my home life. One time a punter gave me two black eyes and left my face in bits. When Patricia saw my eyes the next morning I told her I had been drinking and I fell down the stairs. She probably knew it wasn't true, but she didn't quiz me about it, which I was grateful for, because I had a hard enough time keeping the pain at bay.

When she was 15 she got pregnant and had a baby boy. I looked after the two of them and she left school to mind him full-time. She got pregnant again when she was 17 and had another son. The three of them lived with me and I helped her look after the children. She always was a brilliant mother, even though she started very young. She took responsibility for them immediately and is fiercely protective of them.

She moved out after a few years and went on to have four children. She lives very close to me now and we see a lot of one another. She's with a lovely man and they're building a great life for themselves. I brought her up to be strong and independent; she never took drugs, she only drinks occasionally, and she's a great mother. We get on very well.

Most of the women I knew who worked as prostitutes raised their children very well. The majority of them put money away and sent them to good schools and their children became nurses or social workers; one woman's son is a solicitor.

But some of the women didn't have any self-respect and weren't able to teach their children how to be strong. Consequently their children went off the rails, but they probably would have done that anyway, even if their mothers' weren't prostitutes. The children of three prostitutes I knew became streetwalkers themselves.

You can lose a lot of your self-esteem on the streets. It can be soul-destroying; standing on the side of a road, waiting for a man to come along and buy some time with you. It's a horrible feeling when you really need money and a car drives slowly by looking at you up and down: all you can think about is the £15 that might be driving past.

I always had a very strong belief in myself and I didn't lose that; I fought the negative feelings all the way and I tried to maintain pride in myself. A lot of women went down and became very insecure and depressed; some of them tried to commit suicide.

I remained focused and in control. I found it fairly easy to separate my personal sex life from my professional life. I switched off completely when I was with a punter and I only came to life when I was with the girls. I always got on with the job and did it well. I was very strong. I never lost any of my principles or dignity and I could always hold myself in company; whether I was with a poet or a pauper

During the early eighties I was approached by a member of a well-known drug gang to sell drugs. This man suggested if we both put up £500, we could import drugs from Europe and make a lot of money, but I declined. Making money was always important to me, but I'd rather be a poor beggar than a rich pusher. I saw how drugs had ruined people's lives and it disgusted me to see how drug addicts had such little self-respect, that they wouldn't even use condoms while doing business.

Part of my job as a prostitute involved clashing with the police over and over again. We skirted around the edge of the law and some members of the police really had a thing against the women. I was arrested and charged countless times over the years, but the police never charged a punter caught having sex with me. I began to educate myself about the law and I realised I couldn't be charged on my own.

In prostitution you have to actually see the money being handed over to get a conviction. I fought the police on this point umpteen times in court; I won many cases. The police were mainly charging us for loitering, but when I started fighting the charges, most of the cases were struck out. I went back to solicitor Garret Sheehan and said I didn't think it was fair. How could I be in prostitution on my own? Why weren't the punters being charged? Because the police sometimes didn't follow the correct protocol when they arrested me, I won these cases. Garrett even managed to get a couple of my previous convictions overturned.

Although Garrett represented me time and time again, I never told him I was a prostitute and he never asked. When I was fighting for custody of Patricia, he must have figured it out, but it was really beside the point. Legally I was in the right and that's all that matters in a court of law. In the same courts, however, nothing was ever mentioned about the men. They were always assumed to be gentlemen and that made me so angry. I wasn't in prostitution on my own. The punter should be charged too.

Some members of the Vice Squad were really nice and they got on great with the women. They hated moving on to their next assignment when they would get promoted. The Vice Squad consisted of mainly men, and they worked really hard to keep the women safe.

They wanted to eradicate the pimps altogether and they constantly hounded them. If a man beat up one of the prostitutes, the Vice Squad went to the ends of the earth to get him charged. The streets were more bearable during the Vice Squad tenure; when the Squad was disassembled in 1993, the rapes and beatings rose dramatically.

The Vice Squad still had to uphold the law, however, and they frequently moved us on and tried to stop us from loitering. Sometimes they were very humane, and they understood we just needed to make a living. One time I was sick of being arrested and when two policemen came along I said, 'Ah now, you wouldn't arrest me today, would you? Not after what's happened to me?'

'Why? What happened?' they asked.

'Have you not read the papers?' I asked them.

'No, what's up?'

'My whole bleedin' place went on fire last night. I've nothing left.'

'Okay, we'll leave you alone for tonight and to-morrow night,' one of them said and they went off.

They went mad looking for me when they found out it wasn't true and I had to hide for about six weeks.

In the mid-eighties I was involved in the 'People's Movement for Social Justice,' which represented people from all walks of life. The idea was that all marginalised parts of society would get together and have a voice: there was strength in numbers. There was a huge cross section of society represented including the farmers, housewives, single mothers and so on. Joe Costello represented the prisoners while Cathy and I represented the women in prostitution. Members of Ruhama Women's Project were also there for the women, and Garrett Sheehan was one of the solicitors offering legal advice.

A weekend conference was held and at the end of the first day we gathered for a few drinks. I was talking to someone when a man threw a drink on me and tried to put his hand down my bra to get the ice. I wouldn't let him. I kept taking his hand away and saying, 'There's no ice down there,' while he insisted he would take it out. I was wearing a beautiful salmon coloured silk suit and I didn't want it getting ruined, so I went up to the room I was sharing with Cathy, rinsed it out and hung it up to dry. I was wearing a one piece body suit underneath and I sat on the bed while my silk suit was drying. Cathy followed me when she saw me leaving the crowd and she said she would keep me company. She answered a knock on the door about 10 minutes later. A black-haired, drunken fool barged past her, pulled his trousers down, made a dive for me, and tried to rape me. He had seen me leave and followed me a few minutes later. Cathy helped as I pushed him off, but he was incredibly strong. He was really aggressive and said he wasn't going to leave that room until he got what he wanted. He kept telling me how beautiful I was, and he'd love to go out with me. We both screamed for help and kept on screaming until he eventually got the message and we got him out of the room. We pushed the bed against the door to make sure he wouldn't get back in that night.

The next morning I wasn't in the humour to go down to breakfast. I didn't feel like facing anyone. One of the organisers asked Cathy where I was so Cathy told her I was upset over what happened the night before and filled her in on the events of the previous evening.

The organiser came up to my room like an antichrist to find out what had happened. She was so disgusted at the man's behaviour that she brought me to his colleagues to make an immediate complaint. It quickly became clear his colleagues didn't believe me. We went round and round in circles with the man denying his actions until one of them eventually said, 'Well if he did do that, isn't that your profession?' Despite everything I had seen in life, his answer surprised me and I walked away from them in disgust.

When we came home I didn't bother with anything. I gave up going to the meetings because I felt so disillusioned.

A few years after that incident, Fiona from Ruhama was organising a Mass for the women. A friend of mine who worked on the streets, Róisín, was meeting the priest who was going to say the Mass. Fiona had asked me to go as well but for some reason I didn't want to meet him. Fiona rang me and I told her I'd be over soon, but I stayed in bed. I couldn't rouse myself for some reason; but when Fiona rang again to say the priest was there, I told her I was dressed and on my way over.

Fiona and this priest were talking and happened to get onto the subject of the 'People's Movement for Social Justice.' He told her he had met someone called Tina who had alleged a man tried to rape her at one of the conferences. He didn't know that I was the person involved. He said he heard afterwards the man's colleagues had hushed the incident because they didn't want to tarnish the Movement's reputation. Róisín looked at Fiona and said, 'I'm sure that's what Martina was talking about.'

Fiona asked him about it and he told her a great injustice had been done. When Róisín and Fiona told me about the conversation I knew it was just as well I hadn't met him, because I wouldn't have been able to restrain my anger if I heard why they stayed silent about the assault.

. . .

Although I was arrested on an almost weekly basis, I

usually got away with a fine and a warning. I didn't spend much time behind bars. I was frequently on remand and held in cells overnight, but I never served a sentence for working as a prostitute. The longest I spent in jail was when I was arrested for being the ringleader in the 'Petticoat Gang'. It happened a few years before my mother died and I'll never forget her horror.

The police were arresting us so often that we couldn't work, so five of us went down the country to get a change of scenery. We brought some cans; we were drinking in the car, singing songs, and having great craic. We kept on driving until we ended up in Arklow.

We parked outside a shop that sold stereos and had a big display in the window. One of the girls was so drunk that she smashed the window and robbed a stereo so we could play it in the car, because it didn't have a radio. Another one of the girls helped her carry the stereo into the car while I sat in the back in convulsions laughing at them. I didn't help them to rob it, but I didn't try to stop them. The two girls threw the stereo into the back of the car; the girl who was driving sped off and nearly ran down a garda on the way. The police gave us a 26-mile chase across the country. It was like something out of the film *Thelma and Louise*—it was crazy. Of course they caught us in the end and brought us into Arklow station where they left us alone in a room with just one garda to watch us.

In any other situation the five of us would have overpowered him, tied him up, and then escaped, but when I looked at his hands I got the impression he was slightly disabled and I didn't have the heart to do that. Had he been okay, we would have tied the bastard up and left him, but I gave the signal to the others to leave him alone.

We were all done for theft, but they said I was the leader of the gang. I was sentenced to 12 months in Mountjoy Jail, while the others only got three months each. I appealed my case and got it reduced to six months. My mother was in bits about it; she couldn't stop crying and I had to tell her not to worry. I had received the 12-month sentence so I just had to deal with it. She looked after Patricia while I was gone, which wasn't that long in the end.

I'll never forget Gay Byrne talking about it on RTE radio: 'It didn't happen in Australia; it didn't happen in America; but it happened in a little town in Ireland.'

Mam was giving out about it when she heard the reports on the radio, 'That's disgraceful! What's the young generation coming to where five young girls can do that?' She was even more disgusted when she saw the papers with my name all over them.

chapter seven

Although I was making great money in prostitution, it came with a heavy price. Throughout my many years as a prostitute, I sustained several broken noses, bruises, and numerous black eyes. They became a mundane reality of life after a few months. Prostitutes often have bruises and cuts from being attacked, but they learn how to cover them up and hide the pain from onlookers.

The verbal abuse we received from people surprised me more than the physical abuse. I wasn't doing any harm to anybody—the only person I was hurting was myself. Everybody else tried to hurt me because they looked down on me and called me names. They obviously didn't think I was suffering enough by standing on the streets, leaving myself vulnerable to all types of violence and assaults. The amount of abuse we took off people driving or walking by was unbelievable.

It surprised me to learn that women were even more vicious and nasty than men. I often wondered why women do that to one another. Did they not realise the men gave us a hard enough time? It's as if women were afraid that we'd tempt their men. If a man was willing to pay for sex, then he would seek out and find a prostitute, whether or not she was readily available.

The police also treated us dreadfully when they arrested us. The female officers generally treated us worse than their male colleagues. They called us 'whores' when dealing with us and it was only when the liaison officers, Martina Noonan and Jo O'Leary, came on board that relationships began to improve between us.

I was generally very cautious about my security when I was on the streets but there were occasions, of course, when I made mistakes and got myself into situations I shouldn't have. It's quite surprising I'm still alive today.

A prostitute has to keep her wits about her and follow her instincts if she feels a job is dangerous. Most women develop a sixth sense about punters and can sense if they're safe or not. Mine sharpened fairly quickly after the time I was gang raped in Charlie's flat, and I generally tried to follow my gut feeling on a job. Sometimes, however, I went against my instincts and went off with men when I shouldn't have. Ignoring my gut feelings usually had dreadful consequences.

One night a man came to me looking for business. My instincts told me not to go near him but I needed the money. He looked like a respectable sort; he was wearing a suit and tie, so I told myself that I was being overcautious. I had been working for about two or three years at this stage and I considered myself fairly clued in. We drove by St. Ann's hospital in Dublin 2— there's a church there with a lane to the left of it. We went down the lane and he kept on saying, 'It's a pity. It's an awful pity,' as he was looking at me. When I looked down I noticed that he had a tie in his hand, but he was also wearing a tie around his neck. My whole insides started shaking but I pretended that I didn't notice. The expression on his face had changed and he wore a fixated but distant stare. He had the tie wrapped around his right hand and was twisting it with his index finger. Thinking quickly I said to him, 'Oh Jesus, we're after getting caught. There are two policemen—quick! Drive off!'

He threw the tie down and drove off but he didn't know the area very well, so I said to him, 'Turn left up here. There's another lane here we'll go to.'

I don't know how I stayed so calm and my voice didn't betray my fear. When the car stopped at the traffic lights, I jumped out. I ran down the street and then my legs gave way and I collapsed. Two men that were passing picked me up.

That was an occasion where I nearly died. Assaults were commonplace, but it was only every now and then that I felt close to death. A few years after the incident with the tie, I was working with Dolores Lynch, who was subsequently murdered by a pimp, John Cullen. A punter had pulled up in a car and she asked me to go with her because she didn't trust him. We occasionally would accompany another girl on a job in circumstances like that. Whenever we did, we split the money in half. It was better than nothing because we were still making money.

Dolores had sex with him and when she finished, we got out of the car. Suddenly the man pulled a bar out of the seat and smacked Dolores across the face with it. She got a black eye immediately and I went to grab the bar off him, but he whacked me across the head. I fell to the ground immediately; the bang was inhuman. I was left with an apple-sized lump on my head for three weeks.

Another time I was walking by Burlington Road when I heard a woman screaming from a laneway. I ran down and recognised her as Marie O'Brien, one of the women I worked with on the streets. A man was punching her as he tried to rip her clothes off. He didn't hear me coming; he was so intent on raping her, so I whacked her attacker over the head with my umbrella. He barely flinched as he turned around and gave me an unmerciful punch in the face. I fell back against Marie and knocked her against the wall, hurting her shoulder.

He turned around and walked off, leaving us in a heap on the ground. My jaw was terribly sore and Marie thought she had dislocated her shoulder. After a few minutes we picked ourselves up and went to Gigs to have a meal. We never spent much time nursing our injuries when we were attacked. By that stage getting a hiding from people was par for the course, and although we were physically hurt, it didn't cause any emotional distress. We knew the bruises and bones would heal themselves.

My jaw was sore but it didn't bother me that much. Marie's shoulder genuinely hurt so I said to her, 'Come on up to the hospital and get your shoulder looked at. I'll come with you and explain what happened.'

When the doctor in the Accident and Emergency department heard that I got punched in the face, he decided to x-ray my jaw. He told us that Marie's shoulder was just sprained, but my jaw was broken and I'd need an operation. He booked me in for the next day and sent me home.

The following morning my friend, Lyn Madden, another prostitute, came to to visit me. I had a big corned beef sandwich with her before going to the hospital. She was under police protection at the time because she was giving evidence against Cullen, who was charged with Dolores Lynch's murder. The police that were with her gave me a lift to the Dr. Steevens' Hospital. I thought I was only going in for an examination, but they admitted me then and there. The doctors operated on me the next morning and put wires in around my gums to allow my jaw to heal. They told me that the wires would stay in for about six weeks.

About five weeks later I was sick and tired of having the wires in my mouth. I got a premonition that something bad was about to happen, so one Friday evening I decided to cut the wires before going to work.

That night a punter hammered me. I was doing business with him and for some reason he punched me in the face. He caught me off guard because we were having intercourse and the blow came from nowhere. He jumped up and proceeded to kick me in the face, stomach, and back before he walked off. As he walked away I tripped him up and battered him. Róisín heard the commotion and joined in. The next morning I had two black eyes and a scab on my cheek, which was handy because I was able to pretend to everyone that I fell down some steps.

I went back to the Dr. Steevens' Hospital the following Monday to get the wires removed, but they wouldn't remove them because my face was in bits. I had to wait another week before they'd take them out, but I didn't mind too much because I was able to eat properly since cutting them myself.

After this particular punter attacked me, he beat up another two women, and I felt terrible I wasn't able to warn them on time. We reported the assault, but we may as well not have. The police didn't give a damn about prostitutes at the time.

As a prostitute I was always fighting someone. Not only did we have to fight the pimps and any punters that were violent, we also had to fight against the police. They didn't take our complaints seriously. They also antagonised us by constantly arresting us while we were trying to do our job. I always felt that they would be better off arresting the real criminals— the ones that were stealing cars and murdering people, but they seemed more interested in harassing us.

The prostitutes on the street usually got on very well, but as with everything in life, there were times when we argued. Once pimps got involved it usually ended in violence. One night two of the women, Emma and Róisín, were having a row. Emma was trying to get Róisín to work for her pimp, Declan, but Róisín was having none of it. When she saw she was getting nowhere, Emma got her pimp involved by bringing him down to the canal where I also happened to be working. He started throwing his weight around, telling the women they all had to hand over some of their money to him. I told Emma she wasn't going to get away with bringing a pimp down to control the women. Declan overheard me talking and from nowhere gave me a slap in the mouth. I told him a budgie would give me a harder kick and I turned around and gave him a clatter right across the face. Then I followed Emma as she walked away and told her I wanted to have a fight with her. She wouldn't fight me; this started an ongoing war between us. I resented any man coming onto our beat. They only interfered in our business, took the women's money and frequently ended up being violent towards some of the women. We had enough to deal with on the streets simply by trying to avoid arrest from the police and abuse from the punters.

Another girl who was pally with Emma asked me to go for a drink with her after this happened. She worked on the streets and had never approached me before, so I was a little suspicious of her motives. She wanted me to go to a pub of her choice, but I brought her to my local where members of my family were drinking. My sisters warned me she was trying to set me up, and told me to watch her carefully. I always trusted their judgement and I listened as they warned her off.

'If anything happens Martina because of you, you'll wind up dead. Do you understand?' they told her. The two of us got on well for the rest of the night and decided to go straight to Gigs after the pub closed but she suggested that we go to the canal to get a few punters on the way, because the night was still young and we could make some money.

When we got to the canal Declan was waiting for me; out of nowhere he grabbed a hold of me and started punching me in the face. I wouldn't go down for him out of principal. I held on for dear life and swiped back at him. His friend, Mick, came over and helped him. They started beating me, and although I fought tooth and nail, I couldn't get the better of them. They were killing me but I wouldn't go down for them. Sometimes a person's willpower can give them strength. I was determined they wouldn't get the better of me.

A few minutes went by and I was losing the battle but then one of the women jumped in and pulled Declan off me. As soon as I was released I went over and threw Mick to the ground. Whatever way I pushed against him, he fell down really quickly. I was kicking him and punching him with all my fury and might and he lay on the ground screaming like a woman. Some of the other women joined in and we went crazy on him. All the women were breaking their hearts laughing while he roared for the police to rescue him. A motorbike garda came on the scene, and a man who was watching in a car nearby told the garda that the two men had started attacking me. The garda told the man to fuck off or he'd charge him with loitering. I told the garda about how the two men had attacked me and he said it wouldn't have happened if

I wasn't there in the first place. He gave Declan and Mick a warning and told them to stay clear of the area.

This liaison with the law didn't make any difference to the pimp's attitude towards the women. I was only one of many women that Declan attacked. He knocked women's teeth out and constantly punched them in an attempt to control the streets.

I was absolutely fuming after this incident. Nobody had tried to control me in that manner since I was a child: there was no way I was going to start accepting it now. I made a few enquiries amongst my friends and some of them said they'd help me sort the pimps out. A few days after the attack my friends went down to the canal to sort out Declan, Mick, and Emma. They arrived in a van, armed with a lump hammer and walloped the two pimps until they begged for mercy. While this was happening, two young detectives pulled up. I said to them, 'Just ignore what you're seeing because the two of them beat me up the other night and nothing was done about it.'

I showed them the marks on my legs and arms, and the detectives drove off. Some of the police didn't mind the pimps getting a beating, because there wasn't specific legislation they could use against them, so they often turned a blind eye to this kind of thing. That night my protection group couldn't find Emma and her friend. They were going to teach them a few lessons about working for pimps, but the women obviously knew they'd come looking for them; Emma started working in Ringsend. She left the canal altogether and said she wouldn't work beside me again. Relations had soured so much between us that it didn't bother me in the slightest.

About two or three weeks later I read in the paper that a man had been stabbed near Ringsend. I knew immediately who was responsible for it. The police asked me to make a statement for the time that Declan and Mick assaulted me. They were interested in the assault now that pimps had attacked a member of the public. They wanted me to bring charges against the two pimps helping them prove the men had a history of violence. I told the police to fuck off.

'No, you couldn't give a fuck when it was happening to me, so why should I care about someone else?'

They were going mad because I wouldn't make a statement, but none of the women would. They were all too afraid. It didn't make any difference anyway, because both of them were convicted and sent to jail.

Other pimps were equally as brutal as these two. The name of Monkey McGregor used to strike fear into the heart of any prostitute working when he was around. He was a vicious and evil man who took delight in torturing girls. Anyone that worked for him worked really long hours and hardly ever took a break. One of his girls, Aoife O'Connor, was pregnant and feeling sick so she took a night off and decided to stay at home. When he arrived on the beat and heard this, he went straight up to her house. He grabbed her hands and shoved them into the lighting fire until she screamed and begged him to stop. She arrived down on the beat about an hour later with her hands bandaged up so she could get some punters. Monkey was murdered some time later and the women cheered with joy when they heard the news.

.   .   .

I always wore a long skirt, a white shirt, and a jacket or cardigan when I worked on the streets. I found that I earned my money much quicker in long skirts for some reason. My punters didn't like the girls in short skirts because they found them too trashy. I could never wear trousers because it would have been too awkward. I always had to be aware of not dressing dangerously. I could never wear a scarf, no matter how cold it was; that would be asking for trouble. I never wore shoes with laces and the only gloves I wore were made of leather, so they couldn't stretch.

My punters were always respectable. I wouldn't go with anyone that looked dodgy in any sense. If I didn't like the dirt on the car I wouldn't go with him. My punters were wide-ranging: I had punters from the dole to the Dáil. A journalist was a regular of mine and always gave me great money. He'd bring me out for a meal or drinks every time he came around. He always loved when I wore silk, so I had a few long, silk skirts that I wore whenever I knew he'd be around. I always got around £300 or £400 out of him at a time. He only ever went with me or Róisín because he said to look at us you wouldn't think we were on the streets. He always called us ladies and treated us very well.

One night I went for a few drinks with him and he wanted to bring Róisín and I out for a meal. I went back to get Róisín, but she said she was going to do one more punter before she'd come with me. She went around the back of an office block with him and I waited around the front.

We usually only spent about 10 or 20 minutes with a punter but Róisín was taking ages with this man, so I went in and called her. The man was having problems—he couldn't get it up. When I called Róisín, he came out from around the corner and punched me in the nose. At that moment a taxi driver I knew pulled up and saw what happened. He called me over.

The punter got back into his car, where there were four men waiting for him. They drove off and we followed them in the taxi. Just as we got to Fitzwilliam Square a squad car pulled in. I jumped out and told the police what had just happened. They'd often ignore us, but they had to take notice of me, because the taxi driver was a witness.

The police asked me to identify the man, which I did, and they took him out of the car to question him.

After a few minutes one of the policemen came over to me.

'I can guarantee you £500 in the morning; just leave everything to me. I can get it for you if you don't press charges. If you press charges, we can press charges against Róisín.'

I told him to go ahead, because I knew he had no case against Róisín. He then told me the man's wife would leave him if I pressed charges. He said me if I went into a garda station the next day that he'd have the money for me.

As I stood there talking with the policeman, one of the men got out of the car and said, 'I'll personally make sure that never happens again.' I just looked at him but didn't bother replying.

After a few minutes of discussion, the policeman gave me the name and number of a solicitor and told me to go to him to get the money. I knew then the punter who punched me was a garda, because the two policemen were being so protective of him. They said it wasn't normally like him and he wanted to apologise. I didn't want or need an apology from him but I was happy enough to take his money.

I got an ambulance to the Meath Hospital where I had to sit in the waiting room with blood pumping out of my nose. The ambulance men told the nurses I was a prostitute and they left me sitting for hours. It wasn't even busy in the waiting room; it's just that the nurses were afraid of us.

The doctor x-rayed me and told me my nose was broken, but I knew that before I even saw him. He gave me two painkillers to numb the pain. The nurse gave me some rough, blue paper to wipe my nose and gave me two more painkillers as she told me to go home. I was used to being badly treated in the hospitals, so I went home without putting up a fight or getting distressed.

The next day I went to the punter's solicitor and got £1000 for dropping the charges against him. As I said, I didn't get emotionally distressed when I was beaten, so I was delighted to get so much money for my nose. I had never been offered compensation for any attack on me and it has never happened since.

Of all the injuries I received over the years, facial injuries were the most common and most problematic ones. I'm surprised that my face isn't totally misshapen with the amount of times I broke my nose and jaw.

I sharpened a potato peeler to afford me some level of protection and I used it on punters occasionally. It gave me enough time to run away from a dangerous situation and I'm sure it saved my life. If a punter was attacking me, I'd cut them across the arm or back and while they examined the wound, I ran as fast as possible.

About eight years ago I got my nose broken again. Some girl had robbed a punter, which I hated. It happened occasionally, but I was very strict on the girls who robbed punters because it always came back on us. It increased the amount of violence on the streets, so I always warned the girls they'd have to go somewhere else to work if they were going to carry on like that.

A few nights after this particular punter was robbed, he came to me looking for business. I didn't know anything about the robbery, so I conducted business as normal. He was huge; he looked like a bouncer, but he was well dressed and looked respectable so I gave him a price and we went off to my usual spot behind Leeson Street, at the back of the church. He told me he was too tall to do it in the car, so we got out. He took a lump hammer from his jacket and whacked me across the forehead.

'I was robbed up here,' he shouted as he swung at me. I told him that I didn't do it, but it made no difference. 'I don't give a bollix who done it. I'll get one of you,' he said.

He jumped into his car and drove off. My forehead came out immediately with a huge lump and I couldn't see straight. I sat on the ground for a few minutes, because I felt weak and dizzy. I was tired of going to the hospital, so I got a taxi home and took four painkillers.

I didn't sleep all night and the next day I still felt dizzy and sick. I was at home with Patricia and I didn't want to say anything. I threw the hoover down the stairs to catch my neighbour's attention; then knocked on her door. She rang an ambulance for me and I went to the Mater Hospital.

I told the doctor I fell down the stairs, but he knew I was lying. He kept on asking me what happened but I wouldn't tell him, so he said he couldn't help me if I didn't help myself. I'm not sure why I refused to tell him exactly what happened. I think I was so tired of being discriminated against that I wasn't in the mood for the reaction I was likely to receive. He gave me painkillers and let me go home.

I had two black eyes for eight weeks. I went to the Accident and Emergency department in the Richmond Hospital after a few weeks because I was still dizzy and sick. They told me I had a fractured skull and I had other scars on my skull as well, where it had been broken or fractured in the past. It didn't surprise me in the least because I was always in the wars.

I know I've had a rough time in my life and the scars are on my body to prove it, but in ways I feel incredibly lucky. I survived my childhood where I was sexually, physically, and mentally abused and I survived my years in prostitution. There are so many other women who didn't make it.

chapter eight

Some women didn't make it for a number of different reasons. Some of them died through bad health because they didn't look after themselves properly; others took their own lives; some of them were murdered and more still drank themselves to death.

In 1998 Jennifer McAleer from Ruhama organised a Mass for the women from the streets who had died. We started giving her the names of the women we knew and the list just kept on growing. It transpired that 75 women had died in nine years.

The sad and inevitable thing is that I'm sure there will be many more deaths and murders and I don't know if anyone can stop them. The Legion of Mary had a Mass for the women in prostitution every

November, but we never went to it. We felt it was degrading, because they used to say the women were in Purgatory and they needed us to pray for them if they were to make it to Heaven. I think they're already in Heaven and they don't need our prayers. When Jennifer was organising a separate Mass, I said to her, 'I hope you're not having the Mass because you think the women are in Purgatory?'

'Oh no,' she replied. 'We're just having it because it would be nice to remember the women and to pray for them. They don't need our prayers to get to Heaven.'

.   .   .

One of the women who worked on the streets with me, Nuala Byrne, had a baby girl a month before I had Patricia. She was such a beautiful child—a little picture and everyone doted on her. The baby was tragically killed when the babysitter fell asleep on top of her and she suffocated. It was an accident but Nuala was in bits and couldn't get over it. When I was in hospital after giving birth, Nuala came to visit me and to see my new baby. I felt so bad for her and awkward. I didn't know what to say to her. I remember her saying to me, 'Oh it doesn't matter. I'll be following her in a month, I'll be there with her.'

I told her not to talk stupid, but she kept on saying, 'She's in Heaven, but I'll be with her soon.' I thought it was just the grief talking and I ignored it. About a month or six weeks later Nuala was dead. She was so devastated after her daughter's death that she decided she needed a change of scenery. She was originally from Limerick but had worked in Dublin for years. She was tired of the violence and beatings that were happening on a nightly basis on the streets of Dublin. She figured she'd get an easier time of it in Limerick, because she was local. She was only working there a few weeks when a punter murdered her. He said she was trying to rob him, but Nuala wasn't like that. She wouldn't have done that to anyone because she was very honest and she knew it only increased the violence on the streets when the girls started robbing the punters.

In the trial, her attacker claimed that she was robbing him and he received a light sentence for her murder. Even if it were true and she did try to rob him, it shouldn't have meant he could take her life and get off lightly. I think the main reason behind his lenient sentence was the fact that she was a prostitute. If a prostitute got raped or murdered, nobody took much notice because they said she shouldn't have been out on the streets in the first place.

A lot of women in prostitution were homeless; they stayed in hostels around the city run by the Legion of Mary. These hostels were very strict about their closing hours and if a woman arrived back to the hostel even a few minutes late, they couldn't get in regardless of whether they had anywhere else to go.

A few of my friends stayed in these hostels, but didn't make it back on time once or twice. It had disastrous consequences for some of them.

Teresa Maguire was a friend of mine that used to work the streets. Teresa was always known as Skinny Teresa because she was as thin as a rake. I didn't know her by any other name until she was murdered. She had given up working on the streets, because she didn't want to work as a prostitute anymore. The nuns helped her get out of prostitution and there was no way she was going to go back on the streets for anyone.

We were quite close, because we got pregnant at the same time and we always compared notes about being pregnant. After she got out of prostitution, she was staying in a hostel for the homeless, and one night she got delayed on her way back to the hostel, so they wouldn't let her in. She had nowhere else to go on that freezing cold night, so she went over to the boiler house in Grange Gorman to sleep.

This guy saw her walking alone and followed her. I think he recognised her from the streets, because he tried to get her to do business with him, but she wouldn't do anything with him. She was determined to get out of the business and she wouldn't do it for any amount of money. He got a pole and beat her until her face wasn't recognisable. In fact she had no face left whatsoever. He left the pole inserted in her rectum.

One of the patients in the nearby hospital apparently said he heard a girl screaming, but they took no notice of him because he was a mental patient. The next morning her body was discovered. Her daughter was only three years old; the man served three years in prison.

What I hated most about her death was the way the newspapers degraded her. Even though she had given up the streets, they still referred to her as 'ex-prostitute'; she couldn't escape the tag even when she was dead.

She died on Saturday night, but I didn't find out until Monday morning. Of all the deaths I had seen, this one really shook me up. That night I was out working on Burlington Road and some members of the Legion of Mary came up to us asking us to pray for Teresa's soul. There was a man with them and he said she'd need all our prayers to get out of hell. I just flipped and attacked him; I bashed him about the place. I was so angry because he was still condemning her and wouldn't let her rest in peace.

'How dare you disrespect Teresa like that? That girl is in Heaven and don't you say otherwise,' I sobbed as I lashed out at him. Some of the other women had to pull me off and the Legion members ran off and didn't come back that night.

I never had any time for the Legion of Mary after that. It was ironic that the idea and name for the Legion of Mary came from the premise that Jesus had special time for Mary Magdalene, the prostitute, and they were supposed to help us. In reality they thought they were there to save our souls, and they were convinced we were all going to hell. They'd throw Holy Water over us as we walked by and they were always giving us miraculous medals.

Unbeknownst to them, they sometimes helped us with the police. One night myself and one of the women were walking towards the canal and we saw the police there waiting for us.

'Oh Martina, what are we going to do?' the girl asked. I told her to take out her miraculous medal and I took mine out of my pocket at the same time. As we approached the police, they stared at us, so I said 'Yes?' in response.

They asked us our names so I told them we were members of the Legion of Mary, and we were going to try to talk to a few of the women.

'Oh you won't get any good there,' one of them replied.

'Well, where's there's life, there's hope,' I answered. 'And we'll keep coming down and we'll keep talking to the women.'

They congratulated us both and told us what good work we were doing. They told us we wouldn't get far, but we were great for trying.

.   .   .

Even though the Legion was supposed to be helping

us, some of them didn't really like us. Sometimes we'd offer them a sweet, or a chip and they'd always refuse and say they couldn't take anything off us because it was 'bought with dirty money.' They said we were damning men's souls, but as usual there was no mention about what the men were doing to us.

As I said, the majority of the women died through bad health or drink; but some of them committed suicide when they couldn't take any more. My good friend Judy, who brought me out on the beat that first night, took her own life. She was going out with a soldier at the time and was madly in love with him. They were getting married and she desperately wanted to give up prostitution for good. He didn't know she worked as a prostitute and every night she was out working, she said would be her last. She kept on working so she wouldn't have to worry about money after the wedding, but she was terrified he would find out. She was so excited about getting married, having a normal life and bringing Seán to live with them. A month before the wedding, however, she caught him in bed with another woman and she was devastated. It drove her crazy; she just couldn't cope with it. She was staying in Cathy's flat at the time in Ballybough, and when Cathy was away visiting her auntie, Judy threw herself out the window and broke her neck. She was only 21 years old when she died.

. . .

Another friend of mine, Lorraine Moore, was trying to get out of prostitution by moving to England. She had family over there and was going to start her life over again. She thought if she moved to a new country, she'd make a fresh start. She was going over on a visit before she left for good and was going to organise accommodation and so on in advance of her move. I asked her to bring me back a Fisherprice spider for one of my grandchildren, because you couldn't get them in Ireland at the time. We were talking about her move and she said that she hoped nothing would happen to her, because every time she tried to go to England something went wrong. I told her not to be silly; that she'd be fine.

Lorraine and I worked together on the canal and this particular night I got a bad feeling, a premonition or some sort of sixth sense that told me not to work that night. I was supposed to give her the money so she could buy the toy for me, but I stayed in for a change and watched television. I figured I'd give her the money the next night. This particular night she brought one of her punters to Herbert Park to do business. Lorraine always carried a bit of extra weight on her and he asked her if she was pregnant so she said, 'Yes' thinking that he wouldn't mess with her.

When he heard her confirm that she was pregnant, he thrust a knife straight into her stomach and said, 'That's one bastard you won't have.' He cut her bowel, her womb, and her arteries with one deep cut and ran off leaving her to die.

Another one of the women, Liz, was walking beside the park at that time and nearly bumped into the same man as he exited. He asked her if she was doing business and she told him that she was. She went to bring him into the park.

'Don't bother,' he replied. 'We'll go down that lane.'

As he said that, she got an awful feeling about him and decided not to take the business, so the man went off on his own.

Kate Shaw, another prostitute, happened to leave her car beside the park and as she walked towards the canal, she saw Lorraine lying on the ground. She knew a doctor lived in one of the big houses across the road and she ran across and brought him back to Lorraine. He pressed Lorraine's stomach and administered first aid, managing to stop the bleeding. He saved her life, but she spent two weeks in intensive care afterwards and made a slow recovery.

Lorraine reported the attack and the police took a statement from the girls, but they said it was probably her pimp who attacked her and left it at that. There was no way Lorraine's fellow did it, though. We all knew him and he was a very nice, quiet guy who always looked out for Lorraine. Her attacker was never apprehended.

My former madam, Cathy, came close to death a few times while she was working on the streets. One night a punter brought her up the Dublin Mountains in his car. He beat her up and left her for dead. He left her unconscious, but she came around and managed to make her way back to the hostel in Harcourt Street where she was staying.

She also attempted suicide a few times over the years. The first time she slashed her wrists she was only 18 or 19, but her boyfriend Paul found her and she went to St. Brendan's for a while. A few years ago she tried it again and that time she got help from a kindly nun. She seems to be okay now and she's trying to get on with her life.

One night I went to stay in a hostel where Cathy was staying and I was told about Peggy Flynn's murder. Peggy was a prostitute staying in this particular hostel and she turned up one night with a few drinks on her, so they wouldn't let her in. She sat on the steps outside and picked up a punter who murdered her. She was found strangled on the beach. The hostel was supposed to be a place of refuge and sanctuary but it didn't protect poor Peggy. What was the point in having the place there as a refuge for women, when they left a woman to sit on the steps outside? They didn't care she met her murderer there and continued to bring in other prostitutes afterwards as if nothing had happened. I was only about 17 when I heard about Peggy's murder but I was as strong as an ox and I wrecked the place, because I felt as though the hostel had betrayed her. I vandalised the building that night: I smashed everything that I could—all the big statues, the windows, and everything I laid my hands on. The next day they closed the hostel and never opened it again. The premises were sold soon after.

.   .   .

Whenever there were rapes or beatings on the street and the women reported it, the police rarely listened. They always assumed the pimps were the only ones raping us and beating us, and the police in general treated us badly.

From my first day on the job I knew the police were working against us. I could see the difference in the way they treated shoplifters, or people who robbed houses compared to women in prostitution. The other criminals were spoken to nicely, while the prostitutes were told to, 'Get in there, you fucking whore.' Most of the older detectives, however, were very nice and called us ladies when they spoke to us.

I had been working for about a year before I was brought into a station. A garda arrested me without asking me to move on, which is what they normally did. He came over to us and said, 'What are you doing standing around here?'

'Nothing,' we answered him.

'Right then,' he said. 'You fucking whores! You won't be out here doing it. Get in the fucking van now.'

While they were treating us so badly, they treated the punters with the greatest respect, which was total hypocrisy. Whenever they stopped a punter they took his name and address and said, 'Right then. That's fine. Be careful going with those whores.' People from the dole to the Dáil came down to us so the police had to be careful in the way they spoke to people, because they didn't want to offend anyone that might be 'high up' in society. The women bore the brunt of the harassment and when I saw this happening time and time again, I got so annoyed that I started to rebel against the police. I organised the women and took charge of the streets.

While the police were constantly charging us, they usually left the English women alone and didn't bother arresting them because the police knew the women could just head back to England on the boat the next day. We thought this was ridiculous and we were so frustrated at being locked up for eight or nine hours at a time that we organised gang warfare to get our revenge. Why should the English women be out making money for their foreign pimps while we were locked up, unable to make money to feed our children or pay our rent? I wasn't getting any money off the government, so I had to make a living myself.

There were about 20 black, English women and about 50 or 60 white, Irish women on the beat at the time and every night we attacked any English woman we saw. In fact, we usually just attacked any black woman we saw. We wanted them to go back to England instead of taking our punters and our money. They started going into hiding and the police gave them protection. The punters were being scared away by the continual police presence and business slowed down. When business dwindled the English women went back to England for weeks on end and things started to get back to normal on the Irish streets. The Irish girls were happy with this outcome and we savoured our victory. After a few weeks, however, when all the punters were back, the English women slowly returned to our beat. This gang warfare came to a climax about once a year. For a six-week period the police would generally come along every night and arrest all the women, leaving the English women alone, and the whole cycle would start again.

We made exceptions for some of the English women. A few of them were living here permanently and the police treated them the same as the Irish girls, so we always left them alone.

Some of the first people I met on the streets were English. A prominent English woman, who was later convicted of brothel keeping, was one of the first. She was there around the time of the gang warfare between the women, but it got too heavy for her and she couldn't make any money, so she went indoors. At that stage the streets were being taken over by the black women so we had to put a stop to it. We only allowed a certain amount of them work around

Leeson Street, which is where I was working at the time. I didn't care if they went anywhere else, as long as they weren't interfering in my trade.

In reality most of the English women went home because there weren't that many places they could work. The Irish women had organised Leeson Street and the canal so they couldn't work there. The only place left at that point would have been Benburb Street and they'd rather go home than work there. To be fair to them, at least they wouldn't lower themselves to work on Benburb Street. The Street was the lowest of the low. I always thought the very poor class worked there; the girls who didn't care about themselves. In those days the chronic alcoholics worked there; in the last few years it was mostly run by junkies, but recently they've all moved to other areas, because there are constant roadworks on Benburb Street with the building of the light rail system. The girls who worked in Benburb Street when I was working on the south side were homeless so it was the only place they could get work. They wouldn't have been able to work around our side, because we got mostly hotel jobs and apartments. We'd go off to a pub or nightclub and meet the punters for a drink and then go back to an apartment or hotel.

. . .

Although we did a lot of work in pubs and nightclubs,

we never solicited there because that would have been bad news. We would have been known and barred from everywhere if we did that, so the punters used to ring us and tell us where to meet, and we'd act as if we were just friends. Occasionally the police tried to get us barred out of pubs if they found out we were meeting punters there, which was wrong of them, because we weren't doing any business there. We were essentially two adults having a drink together. If the police saw us several times in the same pub, they'd tell the staff what we were. We used to spread out where we'd go and consequently, I think I've been in every hotel in Dublin.

Occasionally the police picked me up even when I wasn't working. I remember one time I had just rescued a dog and I was going to bring him to a friend's house on the North Circular Road. I was waiting on a taxi and I had the dog by the collar so he wouldn't run off. Suddenly another dog appeared and started to growl and threaten my dog and I knew they were going to start fighting. I had to let my dog go because I didn't want to get caught in the middle of it. While I was standing there waiting on the taxi, the police came along and arrested me for loitering. They didn't believe my story and they threw me into the back of the van with some of the other women they had picked up.

They drove so badly that we were all thrown around the back of the van. I swear they revved and braked and jammed so much; it was as if they did it on purpose. We put a complaint in to the Garda Complaints Board, but it didn't make any difference. It was struck out.

I always stood up against the police and they hated me for it. When I stopped working on Burlington Road and moved onto Leeson Street I was under the jurisdiction of Harcourt Terrace. There was one particular officer in there that clashed with me. We couldn't see eye to eye at all. He thought he'd break me and calm me down, but he never managed to. He brought me to court to get me barred off the streets, but I won the case. He didn't like me because I always stood up for myself and got the other women to stand up for themselves as well. If I wasn't around they'd do what they were told, but I always said, 'Come on everyone. We'll fight the battle,' and they would.

Over the years I led many battles against the police, because besides from the pimps, they were the main people that stood in our way while we tried to make a living.

chapter nine

I was probably the only prostitute who survived without a pimp for so many years. I watched the other women who worked for pimps and they had an awful life. There was one particular girl whose fellow used to smack her with hammers and abuse her nightly. They had to work much harder than us to make the same amount of money. They started work about 9 p.m. and worked through until 3 a.m., whereas I started work about 11 p.m. and finished at 3 a.m. If I was sick or I didn't want to work, then I didn't. If these girls didn't make a certain amount of money, however, they'd be kicked around. I'd see them the next day and they would be too sore to stand. I always stood up to the pimps and fought them. I was always strong. When I saw all the problems the other girls were having with pimps, I resolved never to get one, so I stood up to them when they approached me.

The first pimp to approach me was called Monkey McGregor. He told me I had to work for him. He was renowned amongst the women for being particularly vicious and cruel so I said, 'No! I wouldn't work for you in a million years.' I was on the Burlington Road and I'd been working about seven or eight months at that stage. He threatened to cut me up and told me I'd be found in bits and pieces in the canal, but I still wouldn't work for him. He pushed me around and was very forceful and threatening, but I stood up to him. I'd seen him around and I knew the girls he had working for him, and I wanted to work for myself.

Word got around that I wouldn't work for Monkey McGregor and a few nights later another fellow who was pimping there came up to me and told me I couldn't work on Burlington Road unless I gave him a percentage of my takings. I told him that I wouldn't, so he slapped me around but I still wouldn't give in. This went on for a few weeks where the pimps tried to intimidate me into working for them. When they realised they were wasting their time they left me alone, and I think they grudgingly respected me for being strong enough to stand up to them. I knew life was hard enough; I knew I was taking my life in my hands, but there was no way I was going to take all these risks and get murdered for someone else to take the money.

There was great camaraderie among the women on the street and although I fought with some of them, we all looked out for each other. I worked with two sisters on the beat for a few years, Denise and Rita Egan. Rita was a lovely little girl. Her nerves were always gone because her pimp knew exactly how much she got every night. She had to stay on the canal and do business there, because she wasn't allowed go off in a car with a punter. If she docked a fiver from the night's takings he would beat her; her pimp gave her an awful life.

One night she managed to escape him after work and she went out and spent all her money. She came to me and said, 'What am I going to do? He's going to kill me.'

Another girl called Paula overheard Rita and started making everything worse, so I told her to fuck off and leave Rita alone. She was a bit of a bully and often picked on the weaker girls. When Paula heard me she started roaring and screaming. She went to jump on me, but I grabbed her, forced her to the ground and bit her face. I meant to get her jaw but I got her mouth and wouldn't let go. She was scratching my face and pulling my hair but neither of us would give in. The men gathered round to look but they wouldn't touch us. While the fight was going on, Rita grabbed my fur coat, did two punters and got some money to give her pimp. After a few minutes of rolling around on the ground, I heard someone shout 'the police are coming,' so I got off Paula, took my coat off Rita, and headed down the canal. Next of all I heard, 'Quick, quick!'

I turned around and said, 'What?' This guy was driving alongside me and he beckoned me into his car. He gave me £60 and said, 'That's the best fight I've ever seen. That's what I'm into. Two women having a good scrap; it's the best fight I've ever seen!' If I didn't know how perverted men were before this, I certainly learned that night.

The ambulance had taken Paula to Elm Park Hospital so this man said he'd drive me to see her. I told him I wanted to bring a friend, so we picked up Róisín along the way. I said to her, 'Come on in and we'll give Paula some money, because she has four kids.' Róisín told me Paula's mouth was in bits and she had to get stitches.

I went into see her and I gave her £30 saying, 'That'll teach you now! You can't be bullying the women. You'll have to give it up.' When she got out of hospital she wasn't as bad towards the women again.

We never held grudges against each other, because that's the way the street worked. We fought sometimes, but we always became friends again.

Things changed for me, however, when Máire Geoghan-Quinn, the Minister for Justice at the time, brought in the Criminal Law (Sexual Offences) Act in

1993 which made it illegal to loiter, or to solicit people. All the violence and the rapes came back in and made it very difficult to work. The pimps came back in droves at that point, because the women needed bail and protection money. This Act opened the floodgates to the whole lot and destroyed the way prostitution operated. A lot of massage parlours opened up, because the women started to look at different ways of making money, and wanted to get indoors away from the police.

When the law was enacted it meant any police officer from the local stations could arrest us. The rookies came down to look at us and started harassing us. They were told to keep away from the women in prostitution because we were bad girls, and they were always horrible to us at first. After about six months they'd get to know us and they would be very nice. They'd say, 'Jaysus, we never realised you were such nice people. We were told different.'

What annoyed us more about this Act, though, was that it was sneaked in with the bill on decriminalising homosexuality. I questioned it with TDs at the time and I asked my local representative why they sat there and let it happen. He told me if he had voted against it, it would have compromised the issue of decriminalising homosexuality. I believed homosexuality should have been decriminalised, but I felt they sacrificed us for the homosexuals.

As a result of the Act it became much harder to assess punters before going off in the car with them. God gives us a sixth sense and the women in prostitution have to use it to survive. Other women told me when I first started in prostitution to go with how I felt and to always use my intuition. It didn't matter what way the punter looked, if it didn't feel right or safe then we didn't go, no matter how badly we needed the money, because if we were beaten or murdered then no money was worth it. If something inside was telling me, 'No' and I went with the punter, I usually ended up in hospital. Before that law was passed, if a punter approached a woman she could take her time and decide whether or not she'd go off with him. Now women were taking chances, because they didn't know when the police would come along and they needed to make a living. The women also stopped reporting crimes because relations between them and the police got so bad.

I met a guy around this time through a mutual friend. We started drinking together and he knew what I worked as. I was telling him about the recent violence and how lots of the girls were being attacked. He started coming out with me at night to keep an eye on me. He took the numbers of the cars I went in, and if I went to a hotel he waited around for me until I was finished. I always gave him half of the money I earned, but at the time I felt it was worth it because of the extra bit of security. He worked as my pimp for about three years, but he wasn't my pimp in the traditional sense because I called the shots.

After a few years it quietened down again, because there were so many women being attacked, the police had to step in and start protecting us. A few men were charged with attacking prostitutes and it frightened off anyone who thought they could get away with it. At that stage I didn't need any protection so my pimp and I went our separate ways.

After a few years of the Sexual Offences Act being in place, I had so many convictions for loitering that I got tired of it. I had a criminal record, yet the men that paid for sex walked away scot free. I was fed up with being treated badly by the police. The women were generally treated deplorably by the police and they maintained this status quo because the lower the profile you kept, the less trouble you got. When the women were arrested or questioned, they went quietly. I started to fight back, because it was ridiculous to allow them to do that. The punters were getting away with it and nobody condemned them. Everyone condemned the women: the women were sluts; the women were scum; and the women were whores. When a garda tried to move me off the street by saying, 'Get up that fucking street and move!' I would always refuse:

'That's not a caution! If you caution me properly then I'll move.'

They had to caution me then or arrest me. None of the women were aware of their rights at all because they felt they didn't have any. The law was against them, the police were against them, and the public were against them.

I had educated myself about my rights and the rights of the women on the streets. I had been giving talks to hospitals and been involved in various State projects over the years and my confidence had increased. I knew the women were being mistreated by the police and I decided I wasn't going to stand for it anymore. I told the women about their rights and helped them take cases against the State.

The police rarely charged a punter with me so I took several cases to court. Because I couldn't be a prostitute without a punter, it meant that I won my case a lot of times and it drove the police mad. I felt empowered at this stage and decided to form a union with a few of the women to represent prostitution. Most other professions have unions, but there was no one looking out for us, so we decided to be proactive about it.

We went on the internet to get information on forming a union, because we knew that a lot of foreign countries had unions for prostitutes, and we knew we could connect with them through the internet. We got in touch with some of the sex workers in Amsterdam and made plans to see how they got prostitution legalised. We were going to fight to get it legalised here so we could run the business properly. Prostitution is a time bomb at the moment with the way a lot of prostitutes are using drugs and spreading AIDS.

We looked at the different models that seemed to work in other countries. In Amsterdam, for example, prostitutes need a card to work, and they have to be checked every three months in a clinic. It is also legalised in Germany and the women have a very active union over there. We looked at all the countries around Europe and we planned on taking the best idea from each country and implementing them in Ireland.

At the moment, there is a health clinic in Dublin for the women, but they generally don't go there because of the stigma attached to it. We wanted prostitution to lose it's stigma. We also wanted to get the junkies off the streets. We proposed that any prostitute addicted to drugs or HIV positive should be charged. We knew some of the drug addicts were going without condoms; that was wrong because the men were bringing diseases home to their wives. That really annoyed us, because the wives were innocent as to what was happening.

.   .   .

Most of the police were great when we were starting to organise the union and some of them helped us, but others felt threatened by it. These retaliated by taking our names and addresses every time they saw us. They wouldn't know me by sight but as soon as they'd give my name at the station they'd be told that I was involved in organising the women to stand up to the police, and they'd start to bully me. They often tried to break me down, but they never managed to, so they'd arrest me and bring me to the station. Often they'd come along, arrest me on my own and leave the rest of the women there. I'll always remember the night a garda I'd never seen before came down and took our names. Like the others, I gave him my name and address and he got back into his car and called our names in. He had just pulled away when he swung around and grabbed me and said, 'Right you fucking whore, get in!'

I had a bottle of vodka in my bag and he grabbed it. He then smacked me across the face with it. He threw me into the car and left the other women behind. He charged me with loitering, but the charge was subsequently struck out; but that was the kind of brutality I had to contend with.

While we were investigating the possibility of setting up a union and lobbying the government to legalise prostitution, there was a huge increase in violence against the women on the streets. A number of prostitutes had been murdered and their murders received a lot of media coverage. At this point there was a public outcry at the conditions the women suffered, so the government reacted to this by setting up a committee to enable the police and the women to work together. Things had gotten so bad between the women and the police that there was no trust between us. The women weren't reporting any incidents of rape, consequently the dangerous men were free to continue attacking the women.

Marian McGennis, the TD, approached me and asked me to get involved in the committee. I saw it as a chance to tell the police and government the women's concerns so I readily agreed. The first meeting was in May 1998 and an unlikely crew assembled.

Marian was there as was Superintendent Derek Byrne and Garda Pat Buckley from the Garda Síochána; Sisters Helena and Bríde from Ruhama also attended, with representatives from the Women's Health Project.

I started talking at the meetings about discrimination from the police. I said the police were generally very abusive towards us and the women had no faith in them. The prostitutes thought there was little point in reporting a rape or beating because they felt the police didn't care about what happened. I was always very honest at the meetings and told all the groups about the way things really were. We often got kicked into police vans—even pregnant women would be beaten.

The prostitutes also felt that some of the women's groups only made public statements when something bad happened, such as a woman getting raped, beaten, or murdered, but they weren't there to support us on a nightly basis. We had gotten to the stage where we couldn't take any more, and thankfully this committee was set up just in time.

We told the committee members how we were tired of police from all different districts coming to have a look at us out of curiosity and treating us abusively. We weren't able to tell the police if we were raped or assaulted because we felt we didn't matter. When we started working with the police on this committee we got excellent results. Superintendent Byrne and Garda Buckley were great because they really listened to us and wanted to help. The meetings were held on a monthly basis and relationships began to improve immediately.

One result of this initiative was the Garda Síochána assigning a liaison officer to deal with the women, and Detective Sergeant Jo O'Leary was brought on board. At first none of the women trusted her, because she was a garda, but we quickly discovered that she was really there to help the women. She genuinely looked out for us and she respected us as individuals. After a while the women began to trust her and they were able to tell her about the violent punters or pimps and it started to make a big difference to our safety on the streets.

Another liaison officer, Sergeant Martina Noonan, also started working with the women. She had a very strong personality and we clashed at first. I had a few stand-up rows with her and I didn't give her a chance to work with the women. Eventually Fiona Pryle organised a meeting and the three of us went to a hotel to chat. During the course of the conversation I realised Martina had great interest in the women and she was there because she wanted to help us. I was putting obstacles in her way because I had personal issues with the police, which went back years. I was taking out all my frustrations on her and I realised it wasn't fair. From that moment I decided to work with her and we became very friendly after that; we had some really good times together.

When Sinéad Kelly, one of the prostitutes working on the canal was killed in 1999, it meant the police were able to come to the women and get information on the background to the murder.

I worked on the committee to ensure there was proper communication between the police, the women, and the support groups. The committee took a holistic view of the health and safety of the women in prostitution. If the women were being pressurised by the pimps, we wanted them to be able to go to the police. There were a number of prostitutes on the committee and we took it upon ourselves to help the other women gain trust in the system. The police worked with us to convict the pimps. If the women wanted to leave the streets at any point, Ruhama was on hand to support them and show them an alternative way of life. Everything was working well and it gave the women great confidence, which ultimately increased their safety.

It was great to see how it worked in reality. One time an Irish prostitute was raped by a Bosnian and she reported the attack. The garda who took the details didn't seem too interested and didn't seem hopeful they would catch the man. This woman was devastated. The rape was particularly vicious and the poor girl was in bits afterwards. I brought her up to Jo O'Leary and with her help and encouragement, the woman brought charges against her attacker. Until this point the women didn't have confidence in the police or in the justice system, so they didn't feel it was worth pressing charges a lot of the time. The man got three years for the rape, so it was worth bringing him to court. Cases like that gave the other women confidence and sent out a signal that they were people of value and if they were raped, their attackers would pay for it.

Some of the police, however, had the attitude that if you weren't there on the streets then you wouldn't be attacked. I always pointed out that any woman can be attacked and raped walking down any street. It's not exclusive to prostitutes, and if they didn't make the streets safe for everyone, then the violence would eventually spread. No woman deserves to be raped whether she is a prostitute or not. That point should have been obvious to the police without the committee, but that's what it took to make them understand.

The committee meetings continued and were working well, but then the nuns started organising things for the drug addicts. The prostitutes who weren't on drugs felt they were being sidelined, because the focus and the funding seemed to concentrate on the drug users. The women in prostitution all left the committee at this point.

I lost heart in everything I had been working on when I saw the drug addicts get so many chances handed to them, while the non drug users were left to their own devices. I didn't bother pursuing the idea of the union after that.

．　　．　　．

Although I had great respect for the liaison officers, I couldn't get too close to them or the other police, because I was running a protection racket at the time and making great money out of it. I started off by protecting the women before Martina Noonan and Jo O'Leary were assigned, and I continued doing it for a while afterwards.

I had been through so much and had been taking care of myself for so long that I was well able to protect myself and the other women. I decided if the police wouldn't protect me, I'd protect myself. Other women wished they could be like me. They gradually started approaching me for help, especially the

English women. I said I'd help if they'd pay me and that's how it started.

If anyone threatened or hurt the women, I got some friends of mine to come down and sort them out. I organised the money and I paid them to give certain individuals a beating. I ran the whole scene and I wasn't afraid of the pimps either. Sometimes a pimp would try and muscle in on a girl and take her over when she didn't want him, so I'd get him off her back. If one of the pimps was beating a girl on a regular basis I'd give him the option to either get a beating himself or to stop what he was doing.

I made a lot of money protecting the women—more than I did in prostitution, and it got to the stage where I didn't have to take clients any more. I only took the good punters to keep them happy, but I was mainly there to mind the other women. I spent my nights drinking and the other women let me know if there was any trouble. I got paid for being out there and I collected the money off them. I patrolled the area in a taxi every so often to keep an eye on things.

During this period a reporter rang me and asked if I knew a girl called Tina who was taking protection money. I actually knew this guy very well, but I told him I'd be careful printing that story.

'What do you mean?' he said.

'Well, if you've no proof you'd have a very big lawsuit on your hands.'

'Would you say it's true?' he asked.

'I wouldn't say so. I don't know anything about it.'

. . .

While I was setting up the committee I was also going around the hospitals to try and educate the nurses about the women in prostitution. I worked with Mary O'Neill from the Women's Health Project on this issue. She was also working on behalf of the women's healthcare and their wellbeing. The women were afraid to go into the hospitals and say they were raped or beaten as a result of being a prostitute, because the nurses left them outside for hours. The nurses were afraid of the women and didn't know how to deal with them. They thought we were freaks and they were afraid to handle anything belonging to us.

We had lots of meetings in St. James's Hospital and the nurses were very nice, particularly a nurse called Sandra, with whom I became very friendly. She told us to tell the women they could go there for treatment and they would be treated with the height of respect, just like everyone else. The fact the women couldn't even trust the health professionals really upset me. A lot of the women didn't have family they could talk to about prostitution therefore they were very isolated. They could only talk amongst themselves and you could see the loneliness, fear, and anxiety in their faces. There was terrible isolation and it made me extremely angry; no one cared about us at all.

Even the women's groups began to irritate me after a while, because it sometimes appeared they only looked upon prostitution as a business. There were a few notable exceptions, and we developed great relationships with Sisters Fiona Pryle and Jennifer McAleer from Ruhama. They genuinely cared about us and were brilliant. They've both moved now and unfortunately neither of them are working with women in Dublin any more.

I had a few run-ins with Jennifer at the beginning because I didn't like the idea of her taking over the streets. That was my job and I initially felt threatened by her, but then I realised we both worked in different ways and there was room for both of us. I tend to keep my distance from people so I didn't like Jennifer getting too close. She was coming out too often and bringing different people with her, and eventually one night I got pissed off with her:

'Look, we're not a fucking sideshow. If you're coming out, come out on your own and don't be bringing different people out different nights.'

It annoyed me because you didn't know who you'd be running into. She realised then she should come on her own. We told her not to be afraid, that we'd make sure nothing happened to her. She was brilliant with the women and was very caring and understanding, and once she didn't take over the streets, I found her okay.

chapter ten

If I said that my time as a prostitute was one of the worst times of my life, people would have no problem believing me. If I said, however, that they were also some of the best days of my life, people would probably think I was lying or that I was simply quite mad. Some of my best friends are prostitutes and they really are the best in the world.

When we were working on the streets, we always looked out for each other and for other people. If a woman turned up for work and she was sick, we'd often throw in some money so she could go home. We regularly stopped women getting mugged and raped. We also helped the public. We frequently came across young girls who would be on their own returning from a dance and a man would be following them, so we'd put them in a taxi and send them home.

I remember one particular night there was a girl roaring crying and she came over to us:

'Please, please help me! There's a man following me and I can't get rid of him. I'm afraid of him because he's been following me all night and I don't know where I am.'

'Stand here and we'll get you a taxi and if he comes near you we'll hop on him,' I told her. Sure enough the man followed her down to us and leered at her saying, 'Are you fucking right?'

'What's it to you if she's right or not?' Róisín said to him.

'She's my bird,' he replied. 'What's it to you?'

The girl was sobbing her heart out at this stage and shaking with the fright, hiding behind me. I told her I'd ring the police for her, but she said, 'No, just get me out of here.'

We got a taxi driver we knew to bring her home, and we told him to be careful the man didn't follow him in another taxi. Her assailant lost the head and was very nasty to us, but we were well able for him. He was a real scumbag, though, and he would have hurt that girl.

When I look back on all the hard times I've been through, and the beatings and rapes I suffered as a direct result of working in prostitution, I sometimes wonder how I stuck it for so long. Then I remember all the laughs I had with the women: the funny, happy times we had together. I know some people won't be able to understand that concept; that we could be walking around with bruises and having fun, but we learned to separate our physical senses from our emotional ones.

It was the fun that saved us. The women in prostitution never had any bitterness towards anybody. They never resented anyone for what they had. They were always satisfied with what they had themselves, and they were always willing to give to other people.

We also enjoyed the money we made. We lived the good life and spent our money on clothes, jewellery, and socialising. I never put any money away for the simple reason that no one knows if they're going to be here tomorrow. There's no point in worrying about tomorrow. We often met women and the next day they were dead. Life is too important to waste. We should enjoy it rather than waste it worrying about saving for things. Any of the women who did save money never lived long enough to spend it because their health got them. They either died of cancer or pneumonia, or they killed themselves with the stress of the whole game. Other women got murdered by their punters or pimps. I enjoyed myself every step of the way and had the best of everything. I also spent my money on my daughter and made sure she had the best of everything.

Part of the women's downfall was their good nature. They always tried to please people and this is where they lost out. They would give and give to their pimps until they left practically nothing for themselves; people always took from the prostitutes until they were sated.

. . .

One night just before Christmas, Dolores Lynch came back to us on the canal after taking a punter. 'Look what I got for my troubles,' she said to the group standing around. We all looked down at her hands to see what she got. 'No, my eye,' she said. The punter had smacked her across the face and her eye was swollen and bruised. We couldn't stop laughing, which was dreadful really; but we thought the way she said it was so funny. While we were all standing there laughing, the police came along and arrested all 15 of us. We were furious, because we were just standing with Dolores. We weren't looking for business or anything and we were planning on heading home because it was 5 a.m. It was the night before Christmas Eve and they threw us in a cell for the night; so we decided to make the best of a bad situation and had great fun singing carols all night.

The next morning we started up again, and the sergeant on duty who was releasing us shouted into his deputy, 'Get the Baggot Street choir in here first!'

We were fined £2 each, but we went into the pub afterwards and had a laugh. Dolores's face was in bits for Christmas though—she had a big shiner.

We were always in great mood at Christmas. It was always busy so I worked longer hours. Every Christmas we blew up condoms like they were balloons and decorated the trees around Wilton Place, near Leeson Street.

There was always great excitement when the Vice Squad turned up on the canal. Someone would shout, 'Police!' and the women would all scatter like hens. It was a unique sight. One night when I was working by the canal, the Vice Squad came to arrest us and we all ran off in different directions. I didn't know that one of the girls, Nessa Malley, was behind me and when I stopped suddenly and ducked to hide, she ran straight into me and went flying. She lost her balance and fell into the canal. I was knocked to the ground and by the time I turned around, all I could see was bubbles rising to the top of the water. I leaned over and pulled her out of the canal. As she was climbing out she screamed at me, 'What the fuck were you doing there? You knocked me in, you fucking tramp!'

'You can go back in so,' I said as I let go of her and she fell back in. I ran off down the road and after a few minutes I saw an ambulance heading in her direction. I walked back towards the ambulance and I could see the police with Nessa when I got there. Everyone was being arrested and they were getting ready to grab me, but I said, 'I'm going with that lady,' and I hopped into the ambulance. The ambulance man said, 'Yeah, we'll take the details off you.'

The police took all the women in the van and when the ambulance went around the corner I told them to stop and let me out.

'I thought you were going to the hospital,' they said. 'Fuck off,' I told them. 'I'm not with her.'

I went back and did business while all the other women were in the station and made hay while the sun shone, so to speak.

The women were always getting thrown into the canal so the ambulance men were used to collecting them. Teresa Doyle was the best one at getting thrown in. For some reason the men always threw her into the canal; one night a punter was getting stroppy with her and threatened to throw her into it. She turned around and said, 'Don't bother,' and she threw herself in.

I never did business right on the canal—I always brought the punters off somewhere else, therefore I never got thrown in. If I had to do it nearby, I'd do it in the gardens but I hated being near the rats and the urine. I don't like being anywhere near water, because mad people are always drawn to water and I dealt with enough madness without asking for more.

. . .

Most people couldn't begin to comprehend the

amount of weirdos out there. A lot of men wanted straight sex or a handjob, but we'd frequently get someone who was acting out a bizarre fantasy. Some men liked to pretend they were babies and we'd have to mother them. It's amazing the types of people that are in the world. You'd never see it if you didn't work in prostitution.

One night I was working on Burlington Road when a respectable looking man picked me up. He wanted me to go back to his house, where he said he had a friend staying with him. Normally I would have said no, because it's quite dodgy to go back to someone's house, but I needed the money. We went back to the North Circular Road and went straight up to the bedroom. There was a lamp with a red bulb in the corner so I couldn't see too much, but we got onto the bed and started doing business. After a minute or two a woman came into the room, got into the bed beside us and turned her back.

I couldn't believe it. His wife was lying beside us, but it didn't bother him in the least. I was freaked out and tried to pull away from him but he kept on going—it was obviously how they got their kicks. When he turned the light on, I saw the room was all weird and black, and there were peculiar pictures on the wall that someone had obviously drawn. When I asked who drew them, he told me his wife did.

I started getting freaked out and I told him to hurry up because my boyfriend was waiting outside the door. I told him he always followed me wherever I went, which was a lie, of course, but I couldn't think of anything else to say. Luckily nothing happened and I headed back to the beat where I regaled the girls with the story.

Another time this man brought me back to his house, which was miles out. It was a beautiful big house in a posh area. We were in the bedroom when a woman walked into the room. She was very strange looking with long hair and a really pale face. She carried a hacksaw blade in her hand. I froze when I saw her and she started chanting while looking at me, 'You did it again! You did it again!'

'Oh fuck,' I thought to myself. 'Just play this nice and cool.'

She was in her fifties and looked very sinister standing there with that blade in her hand. I turned around and said to her husband, 'How dare you bring me into this house with your beautiful wife there? Why would you want to do that?'

God forgive me, but she was as ugly as sin. I would have won an Oscar for the performance I gave that night. I played it cool.

'Come here love,' I said to her. 'You can do better than him. Come on and we'll talk.'

She sat down and started telling me she was a chronic alcoholic and her father owned lots of big shops around town.

'I'm sorry love,' I told her. 'I genuinely didn't know. He told me he wasn't married. I wouldn't do that to you. You should get away from him. You're too good for him.'

As she sat there and calmed down, she started crying. I felt sorry for her because he was doing her wrong. I took the hacksaw out of her hands and threw it down the stairs. I was also skirting around trying to get my clothes so I went into the bathroom to get dressed. She was still in the bedroom and he was downstairs. I went back into her and said, 'I'm sorry love, but I really have to go.'

I went down to him and gave him hell. 'You stupid bastard! Why didn't you tell me she was here.'

'I thought she was drunk asleep,' he said.

He gave me £40 for a taxi and I headed back into town on my own, while he stayed with his wife. He came back after that looking for me, but I never went with him again.

I often got punters who wanted to be whipped, and I could never understand how it turned them on. If they ever wanted me to whip them, though, I had no problem doing it. One particular punter of mine loved it when I walked on him wearing high heels. I had to ask if he was a good boy and he'd keep saying, 'Sorry Mammy! Sorry Mammy! Sorry Mammy!' I'd slap the face off him and ask him who the boss was and he'd say, 'You are, Mammy.'

I loved getting the men whose fetish was to clean my house. I always brought them to the flat in Rathmines and if I knew they were coming I wouldn't clean for a few days. It was brilliant. Most people have to pay someone to clean their house but my punter paid £200 an hour to clean my apartment. He got stuck in while I bossed him around:

'Get over there and wash that! Get here and clean that.'

'Yes, mistress. Yes, mistress,' he said as he scurried around cleaning and polishing. He loved taking instructions.

Other punters liked me to insult them while we were doing business and they'd say, 'Call me a whore! Call me a slut!'

While there was an element of danger with any punter, one of the most dangerous types was the religious punter. We often had priests or religious freaks coming down looking for business. I was in the car with a punter one night giving him a handjob. He wanted oral sex and I wouldn't give it to him. It's one thing I wouldn't do, no matter how much money was offered. He kept on at me and I said, 'Look, I don't do it, but there's another girl that does, so we can work together.'

I called Eileen over and I asked her if she would perform oral sex on him. She agreed and got into the front seat while I was in the back. I told him he could feel me while she was giving him a blowjob. He paid for it and everything was going fine until he climaxed. Suddenly he started to roar and cry, 'I'm after abusing you. Oh God! God forgive me! God forgive me!'

I panicked because those religious freaks are very dangerous. I said to him, 'You're okay; you're okay. Eileen, get out. Open the door.'

We got out of the car slowly and left him there sobbing crying, because men with religious issues can turn on you and kill you very quickly.

That's why I have so many issues with religion. One minute the priests were judging us and calling us sinners; the next minute they were turning a blind eye to rapes, while other priests were clients of ours. It was all very messed up. Sometimes people from religious orders tried to demean me; speak down to me because of my profession, but I never let them. I believed that they could be the biggest perverts behind closed doors. I hated anyone who represented religion for years, because I felt as if they judged women in prostitution on their moral standards, and judged other people on their wealth. You might have a little bit more money than other people, but no one is better than anyone else. A lot of the priests and religious orders didn't care what people did behind closed doors, as long as they maintained respectability on the surface.

Of course I like certain members of the religious orders, and some of them have become good friends of mine. I have great respect for Sister Fiona Pryle, who worked in Ruhama while I was on the streets, and we became friends over the years. One of the things that I liked about Ruhama and the nuns that worked there was that we never had to address them as 'Sister'. They put themselves on the same level as us, and we could relate to them a lot easier that way.

I did go off with a preacher one night though. My arm was in a plaster cast for a few weeks, because I had cut my finger off with a broken glass and it was sewn back on. I had to go back working with the cast on, and this particular night I was wearing a beautiful salmon coloured silk suit with my plaster on underneath. We were all there on the beat when a car pulled up and a man walked straight over to me. I went crazy and said, 'What the fuck are you coming over to me for? Is it because I have a plaster cast on? You can fuck off if you think you're going to mess me up!'

'No,' he said. 'I'm a Christian,' and he ran over to his car and showed me all the bibles he had in his boot. He said he wanted to save our souls, and every night after that he would stand there singing holy songs with some of his friends. They used to sing the *Lord is Thine* and all that type of thing, but I'm not sure what religion they were. Some Chinese people were with him singing, and he was definitely a preacher of some kind. Every time I hear Dusty Springfield singing *Son of a Preacher Man* it reminds me of him.

Their singing drove us mad, so I decided I'd fix him. I brought my big stereo down to the canal and blared out chart music. After a little while we saw the police coming, so I hid the stereo in the bushes and switched it off. The police said they got disturbance complaints. We told them it was the religious crowd, so they got them to stop singing.

They still came back every night, and one night when I was bored I said to the preacher, 'How strong is your faith?'

'It's very strong,' he said. 'It's strong enough to walk across that water.'

'Right girls,' I said, and with that I pushed him into the canal. He sunk like a brick. He told the police I tried to murder him, so the police told him not to go back on the beat, and he should probably give up trying to convert us.

A week later I was on the street on my own when he pulled up to ask me to go for a meal with him. During the meal he asked, 'Are you going to do business with me then?' That's what he was after the whole time, so he booked a room in a hotel, gave me £250 and brought me out drinking.

I stayed in the hotel until three in the morning and then went to Gigs to meet the other girls. I told Róisín what happened; she said she knew he was going to approach me because he was always watching me. Going with him was the only way to get rid of him. He couldn't show his face on the canal again.

Another time I got this punter who was extremely nice and gentle—too much so. There was something about him that I couldn't put my finger on. Anyway, I opened the glove compartment to get some tapes out and all his things fell out, including a bible and collar. When I saw he was a priest, I didn't want to be with him any more.

I asked him to drop me back and he asked why. I told him I'd prefer it if he dropped me back. He said, 'But you haven't finished me.' When I told him I wasn't going to finish him either he lost his temper and punched me in the face. Then he started panicking and saying, 'I'm sorry, I didn't mean to do that.' He dropped me off and I never saw him again.

. . .

Of all the punters I had, I never once felt anything for them, other than a desire to make money. Some of the men wanted more from me and a lot of them asked me out on dates, but I'd only go if they'd pay for my time.

I had a few regulars and this suited me fine, because they always treated me well and I knew what to expect from them. One time, however, a man who used to be a regular of mine started following me around. He wouldn't take no for an answer. I started telling him I was too busy when he wanted to do business, but he wouldn't accept that. He ran after me with a butchers knife one night, so I got a barring order against him. Any time I saw him after that, I jumped into a taxi and got out of the area. I stopped working on the canal at that point and moved onto Fitzwilliam Square.

He didn't bother coming around after that because he knew I wouldn't go with him no matter what he offered me. After that I made it a policy of mine never to go with a punter more than five times. Most of the violence on the streets was with regulars, because they thought they owned the women. They thought they were buying the women; that they became their property. I kept one or two regulars that I knew very well, but I kept everyone else at arms length.

I'd often see my clients if I went drinking, but I wouldn't acknowledge them because I never knew who they were with. One particular punter brought his wife to see me on the beat and that drove me crazy. I had been with him about three or four times when he brought his wife to the canal and pointed me out to her. She just smiled at me and they drove off. I got used to people's idiosyncrasies and I learned not to assume that any one person was 'normal.' There is no such thing as a normal person—normality is only something that people are used to.

Another punter of mine loved it when I robbed him. I did it to him so many times he must have realised what I was going to do, but he always came back for more. He came to me looking for business and asked if we could spend the night together. He said he'd give me two or three hundred pounds for my time and we did business a few times. I always brought him back to the flat I rented with some of the other women. I'd only spend about an hour or so with him and then I'd say, 'Come on. I'm hungry, let's go for a meal.' We'd go out and I'd spend the night dancing and ignoring him. Another time he came out with me but I told him I was going to the toilet and I climbed out the window. He soon realised my game and one night he said he wasn't hungry, so I got a taxi man I knew to pretend he lived in the flat. He walked in on us and pretended to go mad so my punter had to leave.

.　　.　　.

I saw all types of fetishes during my time as a prostitute and it always amazed me to learn what turned people on. Some people were so kinky and took it so seriously that I had to laugh, but they were always great for making easy money. My favourite punter was a man who used to stuff a pillow up his jumper and pretend he was pregnant. We had to imagine we could feel the baby moving and the more we told him it was moving, the more money he'd give us. I used to say the baby was practically dancing out of his belly. He would say, 'Oh, I'm after having terrible sickness this morning,' and I'd say 'Oh you didn't, God love you. It's terrible, isn't it?' We'd sit in the car talking about the baby; that's all he ever wanted. He never wanted sex or anything like that.

We often got transvestites coming to us simply for chats and company. We always brought them to our rented apartment where we'd sit in comfort with them putting on make-up and talking about women's issues. This was in the eighties when there wasn't really anywhere for them to go and dress up; so they'd come to us. We always had great fun with them and it was one of my favourite jobs. They'd bring their girly clothes in a bag and get changed up in the flat. Once they were inside they'd put on their skirt, suspenders, stockings and bra. They loved trying on new underwear and we had to tell them how good it looked on them. Sometimes we'd try it on for them, so they could see how it looked on a woman; it was great, because they always bought good quality underwear from Brown Thomas. It was better quality than any of mine. They often gave us lovely underwear to keep because they used to say it looked better on us.

They never wanted sex. We used to call them Josephine or Georgina or whatever, and help them put on their lipstick or teach them how to put on their own make-up. I'd put on their mascara or do their eyebrows for them. We'd drink coffee and chat about girly stuff. We always had a great laugh with them. I had to be careful never to laugh at them, though I nearly did on many occasions, especially when they'd start talking about their periods. They used to come out with outrageous things saying they had terrible cramps. I would play along and tell them to take half a Codeine because it was great for period pain.

The prostitutes were more like social workers for the cross dressers. Some of them would start crying and tell us their wives left them because they couldn't handle their cross-dressing, so we'd advise them on what to do. I felt sorry for those men because they couldn't help it.

Other times we got perverts who wanted to do threesomes. I got a couple once where the girl wanted to do a lesbian act, but I'd never do that, so I told them there was another girl who would do it. The man then asked if I'd go with him, which I had no problem doing, but I got Siobhán, a lesbian, to go with his girlfriend. They paid us £150 each for the session. We went up to the flat and the girls took the bed while I went on the floor with the man. He was watching her while having sex with me, and they seemed to have a great time. We got lots of requests for threesomes, but I'd never go with the women, I only went with the men.

One time I got caught terribly by a punter. There was a man across the street and he kept calling me over, so I told him to come over to me. I'd never cross the street for a punter—I always made them come to me. He asked how much I charged and I told him it was £15 for a handjob and £25 for sex, but I wouldn't do oral sex. He said a handjob was fine so we went into the park. He asked could he feel my chest and I told him that was fine, so he gave me £20 and started feeling my chest.

'Come on,' I said, 'you better take it out.'

'No, not yet,' he said.

I put my hands down and there was nothing there. It turns out that it was a woman; she must have been a dyke but it was impossible to tell. She was wearing men's clothes and looked just like a man. I screamed so loudly with the fright that the other women thought I was being attacked and ran over to me.

.   .   .

Sometimes there were peeping Toms that hung around the canal and masturbated themselves while they looked at us and called us over. They were dirty scumbags though. There was one particular man who was on the canal every night of the week. He called us by going, 'Whoo-hoo!' and he wanted us to catch him at it. We decided we'd put a stop to him so one night five of the women stood at the top of the canal while six of us walked down towards him. He didn't see the five at the top. The group of six walked by him ignoring him while we talked and he called out to us, 'Whoo-hoo!' while he flashed at us. We turned around and chased him up the canal. When he got to the top the five women were waiting for him and they grabbed him, stripped him naked, and threw his clothes into the canal. He never came back.

There was another man that hung around the canal and he was the dirtiest person I've seen. He walked around picking up the used condoms and to this day I have no idea what he was at. He sickened my stomach just looking at him, because he wasn't doing it out of a civic duty to keep the canal clean. Some of the women discarded the condoms wherever they had sex, but I always carried tissues with me, and the men would wrap the used condom in the tissue and dispose of it later.

.   .   .

We loved winding the police up and did so at every opportunity. Whenever they'd bring us into the stations, we'd go in the back door and march straight out the front door. We would hide in the gardens to get away from them. One night, the detective on duty realised what we had done and he chased me through the station and up the road. There was a man on a motorbike at the traffic lights and I ran up to him saying, 'Quick love. Can you bring me to a garda station? That man is trying to rape me.'

He told me to hop on and he drove off. He pulled in after a while and asked me which garda station I wanted to be dropped at and I replied, 'That's grand. You've just taken me from it.' He got the fright of his life and drove off in a hurry.

The next morning I went down to the Bridewell courts to see how the girls were getting on. The detective from the previous night put his hands out to grab me and I said, 'Don't even think about it. You're looking for a promotion and how do you think it'll look if you let a little thing like me get away from the station? Your promotion would be gone down the drain.' He let me go, but he hated me after that.

After that night they installed digital locks on all the doors, and we didn't know the numbers so we couldn't escape. It wasn't too bad when Sexy Sergeant was on duty though. He always had a bottle of vodka in his room. Róisín, Denise and I would run up to him and we'd sit there drinking vodka with him while Denise gave him a handjob. The other police would leave us alone while we were with him and we had a great laugh with him.

When I was out on the streets, he used to come around to see the women. He'd let me take a punter down a lane for business and give me about five minutes with him. Then he'd follow us down and say, 'What's going on down here?'

The punter would panic and say, 'Hold on a minute, guard, we're not doing anything.'

'You get the fuck up there,' he'd say to the man and then he'd turn to me, 'and you wait here until I've finished with your man.'

He'd come back to me and say, 'Go on—give us a look.'

I'd have to lift my top and give him a look at my breasts, and he'd go, 'Ah Jaysus, don't do that. Go on, give us another! Give us a look at your legs.' That's why the women used to call him Sexy Sergeant.

He always warned us when the Vice Squad were on their way around. We'd hide in the bushes and when the Vice Squad would arrive, there wouldn't be a sinner around. They couldn't figure out where we'd gone.

The funniest thing I saw in a station one time was when there was no room in any of the cells so they put six of us in one of the offices. One of the women, Miriam Fitzpatrick, opened the press and discovered a pile of fox furs, the ones you wear around your neck. Miriam walked out of the station with two of them hanging around her neck and none of the police even noticed.

Another time there were five of us waiting in an office where there was a box of tracksuits that had obviously been stolen and recovered by the police. Unfortunately they were stolen once again, because we each took a tracksuit and put them into our bags; we laughed our way out of the station when we were released.

We even managed to have a laugh sometimes when we were in court. I was in Bridewell Court once and I was annoyed because I had been arrested three times in the past week. I refused to recognise the court, because I knew I'd be found guilty even if I pleaded innocent.

'There's no point in pleading, your honour,' I said 'because you're not going to believe me anyway.' When the judge heard I wasn't recognising the court he said he'd put my plea down as 'not guilty' and he carried on with the case. In the end he found me guilty, as I had predicted. The next day I was in court again with another girl from the streets and this time the judge said he'd put us down for a weeks remand in Mountjoy. I asked him if I could have bail.

'And why should I give you bail?' he asked. 'What excuse do you have?'

'Well, I have a child, your honour.'

'Have you now?' he asked as he took his glasses off and started polishing them. 'Well that's just as good an excuse as any,' he said looking at me. 'And you, Mrs. Murphy, what excuse do you have?'

'I'm a deserted wife with four children.'

'Well that's a very good excuse,' he said as he continued to polish his glasses. 'Get down those stairs now. I don't care if you're running an orphanage between you. Bail refused!'

I wouldn't have been able to continue in prostitution if I didn't have these good times to balance the bad, because when you have a bad day as a prostitute, you're at risk of either ending up in jail or dead.

chapter eleven

I was arrested countless times for assault and disturbing the peace. A lot of the police didn't like me, because I was so outspoken. They found me very hard to deal with because I always roused the women and made them stand up for themselves. Some of the police were decent men and they tried to help me in different ways, but others just couldn't wait to arrest me.

A sergeant in Store Street was lovely and he was always asking me to get counselling. He could see I had pent-up anger and I could be a better person if it was managed properly.

'Martina, you're very stressed out, you know. I've never seen anyone so stressed out in my life,' he said to me one night. 'You're constantly on the defence and you run these streets. You rule the women and you'll die doing it if you're not careful.'

'I don't care,' I retorted. 'If I'm born to be hung, I won't be shot.'

'What happens if you get a man that kills you?' he asked. 'What will you do then?'

'I couldn't do anything if I were dead, could I?' I asked him and he just laughed.

He offered to pay for counselling sessions for me, because he said I was one of the worst cases he ever came across. He knew I wouldn't back down for anyone—pimps, punters, or police and he thought it would get me into serious trouble one day.

My wilfulness and temperament got me into plenty of trouble, especially when I rubbed certain policemen up the wrong way. One particular garda had it in for me, because I would never go quietly with him when he arrested me. He swore he'd get me on something before he left the beat. The week he was finishing up, he started hassling and bullying me. I couldn't take it any more so I ended up pushing him back and smacking him across the face. He charged me with assault and it was my word against his so I lost the case. The judge didn't believe I was acting in self-defence, because the garda swore he didn't touch me. I was fined £100 and bound to keep the peace for two years, but at least I didn't go to jail for him. I never bothered paying the fine either.

.   .   .

Whenever we were arrested, we were always brought to Court 44 in the Bridewell, and I got to know the inside of that courtroom intimately. Occasionally a punter was charged with us but they were always processed separately to the women. Most of them got away with a warning and were sent on their way. The men were never brought in with us, which I always found strange. We were never sure if they actually went to court because they were treated so well in comparison to us.

During one period I was brought to court eleven mornings in a row. I was in front of Judge O'Leary the whole time and it got to the point where he asked me if I was the only woman working the streets. He kept throwing the charges out of court, because there wasn't enough evidence against me. The police used to arrest me whenever they could get their hands on me, but they weren't charging me with legitimate offences.

The eleventh time I was arrested, I gave the Bridewell as my address, because I'd spent every night there for the previous ten nights. The police tried to do me for using a false address, but Judge O'Leary, who was a great judge, said I had every right to use that address because I'd been staying there every night for the past two weeks.

Some of the judges were okay, but some were bastards to the women. There was a lot of discrimination in court, and the judges mainly sided with the police. There were occasions, however, when they believed what I said. One time I was in a garden with a black man and the guards came along and arrested me. They let the punter go, but they took me down to the station. We weren't actually doing anything—we were only talking about a price and then we were going to go to a hotel. When the guards came, we hid in the bushes, but they found us.

In court the next day, the garda said he arrested me off the bridge, so I interjected at this point, 'Your honour, he's a liar. I wasn't off the bridge.'

'Just call me a liar again,' the garda warned me. The judge peered down at me from the bench and asked, 'Well, in all honesty, where were you, Martina?'

'Your honour,' I said. 'He arrested me in a garden with a black man.'

'Is that so?' he asked, and he threw the case out.

.   .   .

I co-operated with the police only to suit myself. I never gave a false address because there was no point. They were able to check it out fairly quickly and it would only bring extra trouble upon myself. One night when I was brought into the station, it was filled with prostitutes. I said to the detective on duty, 'This makes me laugh. There must be no crime in this town if all you have to do is pick up the women.' The next day in the paper there were the usual reports of muggings, thefts, and assaults but none of those people were held overnight in a cell. The police were too busy chasing the women to catch the real criminals that were causing trouble on the streets.

When we were arrested, whoever got away from the police had to bring burgers and chips to the women prisoners in the station. One night I escaped while the rest of them were arrested, so I bought a big bag of burgers and chips and brought them down to Harcourt Terrace. I was climbing in the window when I heard a voice from behind me, 'There's no point in you doing that now, Martina. We can bring you in the door.'

One of the detectives was standing there laughing at me and he brought me inside, where I was locked up with the rest of the women. It was comical. I couldn't stop laughing and it was probably the first time I didn't mind being brought in. They hated when we got one up on them, and yet that was partially how I got my kicks.

I hid everywhere from the police—under bins, along the canal, in the bushes—anywhere and everywhere. I built a bunker beside the canal and this was where I usually hid. I had covered it with leaves and it just looked like a bush from the outside. It was a perfect hiding spot until I got caught because of Natalie Byrne.

One night at work I knew the police were in the area and I hid in my bunker. Natalie was one of the women who worked on the streets and she walked slowly along the canal and stopped outside my bunker looking for business. After a minute or two the police came along in plain clothes, but she was looking out for the vice squad so she didn't realise they were detectives. I couldn't warn her, because they were too close and they would have heard me. Everyone else in the vicinity had scarpered, so the canal was empty all of a sudden.

The policewoman said to Natalie, 'How's business?'

'What's it to do with you? Mind your own fucking business!'

'I'm a copper,' she said.

'Are you?' Natalie asked. 'Well, if you're a copper, then I'm the fucking vice squad.'

She pulled the detective down by the hair and kicked her. I started roaring laughing, because Natalie thought she was messing with her. I was laughing so much I didn't hear anyone come up behind me. Next of all I heard, 'Come out you!' and another garda took me out of the bunker and down to the police station.

They arrested Natalie as well and in the end she was charged with assault, but she wasn't charged with assaulting a police officer, which carries a much heavier penalty. The policewoman hadn't shown Natalie her I.D. so Natalie couldn't have known she was a policewoman. It meant that Natalie escaped with a lighter sentence.

. . .

I worked on the streets never thinking about tomorrow. I never saved money for a rainy day, because I never knew if I would be murdered when I went out to work at night. I saw some of the women deteriorating in front of my eyes. The streets ate their souls away, but I wouldn't let it eat mine. I had an inner strength in me and I'm not sure where I got it, but I knew I would always be okay. I was like two different people when I worked out there. During the day I did the normal things women and mothers do. I washed clothes, cooked dinner, got my hair done, played with the children and kept everything in order. At night time I started to psych myself up for the evening ahead, and I became defensive and aggressive. I got into work mode, where I could approach anyone and look for business and yet be able to take rejection if the punters chose someone else over me.

When I was about 19 and working in the business a few years, this youngish boy came down to the beat looking for business. The streets were fairly quiet that night, and I was delighted with myself as I sauntered up to him, because he was around the same age as me. 'Nice one,' I thought to myself. 'This will break my luck.' I was all dolled up in a suit, but he walked straight past me and picked up a woman we called 'The Gonk.' I couldn't believe it. She was in her fififties, very severe looking and had her hair pulled back in a bun. He was lovely looking and I couldn't believe he picked her over me. While they were off doing business, the police came and caught them, and even they couldn't believe a lovely looking boy like that would go with her. All tastes were catered for on the streets.

. . .

Jennifer from Ruhama came around to us one time and asked what the women needed from the project and how could it help improve things for us. We told her an education course would be good for the women because a lot of us had skipped most of our schooling because of our backgrounds. She genuinely wanted to help the women and she listened to what we had to say. We told her that no woman should be allowed in the Ruhama building if she had drink on her, because we wanted somewhere we were safe from drunkards. It would also help the women to take the work seriously.

At the beginning it worked very well, because the staff there were lovely and worked for the women. Fiona had the place really homely; it was a sanctuary for the women trapped in prostitution. I did my Junior Certificate in Ruhama and I spent about two years doing courses with them. I got honours in Art and English, and I was delighted to be on a learning curve. When I did my Junior Certificate I was in a class on my own, which was very boring. I couldn't compare notes with anyone about the course content. They said the women wanted it that way, but they didn't really. Ruhama spread the classes out and it looked as if there were lots of women taking classes there, but in reality there was only a few.

As part of my art class I did a big painting that was hanging on the walls there. It was presented to the President when she visited the centre. Various gifts were brought up to her as a symbol of the Ruhama project and my painting was one of them; I was so proud of that.

.   .   .

I never went to Ruhama with the intention of leaving prostitution. I didn't think they could ever offer me an alternative. Fiona convinced me I could leave the streets and start working in something else if I really wanted to. She did it in her own time and we had many conversations about the future direction of my life. She saw a lot of things in me I hadn't seen in myself. She saw that I was very good with animals; that I always looked after them and minded them for other people. I often had baby kittens and would syringe feed them and mind them until I found them good homes. She said to me, 'Martina, you have a great gift with animals. Would you not go and do something about it?'

So I went into animal rescue and I now do my own rescue service where I foster animals and rehome them. I also did another art course and I did very well at it. I was studying hard and getting more and more into animal rescue work. I found it hard to continue working on the streets while studying, so I only went out at weekends. I had my regulars and I met them in their apartments or in hotels. When I finished, I went to Gigs with Róisín and everyone, and we'd drink 'till seven in the morning.

It was while I was doing the course that something started stirring in me. I felt there was something ahead of me in life outside of prostitution. I wanted to get off the streets. It was early 1999 and I wanted to leave everything behind me and make a clean break of it. I wanted to work with animals and I knew I could make a living from something other than vice. Until that point I thought I'd be a prostitute forever. Once I made the decision I stopped overnight. There was no point in thinking about it too much, because I knew I'd keep finding reasons to stay working in prostitution. You get addicted to the money and you think, 'I can only get this if I'm working on the streets,' or 'I can go out one night and get treble what I'd get working in a "normal" job.' I got out of it straight away, mainly for my grandchildren's sake.

On my last night I went to Gigs as I normally did and had a good meal and a few drinks. I didn't tell the others I was leaving, because I didn't really know myself then. I wasn't sure I'd be able to stay away, because there's always the chance if you're stuck enough, you'll go back. Prostitution is an addiction. Women get addicted to the money and it's hard to give up. A lot of women would say, 'I'm giving it up tonight and I'm never coming back,' and they'd leave. Three months later they'd be back out.

I never say never, because I've seen it so often, but it's four years now since I stopped and I've never gone back. There have been times, though, when I've struggled financially, that I've been tempted.

I feel much better now that I'm not working on the streets. The most obvious improvement in my life is that my health is much better. I was always getting pneumonia because I've got asthma. I used to get pneumonia on a regular basis when I was working on the streets. I remember working one night and I drank a bottle of vodka because I was feeling so bad, and I was trying to numb the pain. The sweat was pumping out of me while I was talking to one of the girls so I sat down but I couldn't get back up. One of the girls brought me to the Meath Hospital and the doctors wanted to keep me in, but I had nothing arranged so I wouldn't stay. The girl who brought me to the hospital ran off with my clothes and left me with none to make sure I couldn't leave. It was just as well, because I was very sick.

Another time I had viral meningitis and I ended up in the Hospital once again. I was out working at the time and I didn't know I had it. I was unbelievably sick with it, but I thought it was only a migraine, because I suffer from migraines anyway. The headache was unbearable and I was really pale, but I carried on working. I don't know where I got the strength from. I was swallowing painkillers by the packet. A day or two later I was at home in bed and Jo O'Leary rang me to ask me if I knew anything about a rape that had taken place.

'Jo, I wasn't out because my head was lifting,' I told her.

'You sound dreadful,' she said. 'Ring an ambulance, because if you don't, I will.'

I got an ambulance to the Mater Hospital and I stayed there for 21 days. I thought it was a bad migraine so I had struggled on. They did a brain scan because they thought it was a tumour and I got the fright of my life. I was there on my own and they did a lumber puncture which showed it was viral meningitis. Once I was admitted, they treated me extremely well and acted fast, but I was waiting on a trolley for 17 hours in the outpatients department. There were lots of drunken people on the floor outside my cubicle vomiting and roaring; it was dreadful. I felt so degraded to be stuck in a room with all these winos and drunk people, especially when I was feeling so bad. Luckily I recovered and I haven't had any serious health problems since.

. . .

Around the time I did the Junior Certificate, I started looking into getting counselling. I had sought help years previously, when I was only about 20, but I came to the conclusion it was a waste of time. Róisín had been doing it and she kept on saying how great it was, and how it worked for her.

One time I went with her to Stanhope Street and she came out sobbing. 'What the fuck did she do to you?' I asked. I was going to go in and find out why she made Róisín cry, but Róisín started laughing and told me what happened. A few of us went with her after that and the nun always gave us a big tray of biscuits and tea to keep us quiet. I think she was afraid of us when she saw how worked up I got on the first day.

We didn't understand the counselling process and how it opened wounds. Róisín always said to me, 'Martina, please go. It'd be great for you.' I always said, 'No way! Fuck that, if that's what it's doing to you.' I wouldn't take counselling because I probably wasn't ready for it then.

Years later as I began to mature I felt as if counselling might be good after all, so I asked Sister Jo from Ruhama, who was lovely, if she would counsel me. She was a qualified counsellor and we were talking about counselling one day with her so she said she'd do it for me. Then her father was taken ill. Every week she'd tell me she'd take me when she had more time. Then her father deteriorated, so I said to Fiona, 'I wouldn't ask her to counsel me now. She has enough on her plate without having to listen to me.'

I asked Fiona to get me a counsellor, but it would have to be someone I liked or I wouldn't be able to go through with it. It wouldn't have mattered how good they were; if I didn't click with them, it wouldn't work for me.

So Fiona organised a counsellor and told me I would like her; that she was very good. Funnily enough when I met her we clicked. I've been going to her for a few years now, and if I'm not in the mood for a counselling session, we'll go for a cup of tea and I like that. I like the way she's flexible with the counselling. I find I can come to terms with a lot of things since I started.

I deal with life a lot better now; there was a time I didn't know how to cope with it, but now I have certain mechanisms and I'm very self-aware. We talk together and I direct the topics of conversations in the sessions. She's very good because she cares about people; she does a lot of counselling for women in prostitution. It has helped me an awful lot. It helped me to deal with things, to manage my anger, and to cope with life in general. I would recommend anyone to get counselling. Dublin Corporation should bring it into areas where they have a lot of council housing, because there are a lot of women living in the flats who have a lot of stress with their children, money problems, partners, and alcohol abuse. If they were offered help, I think they would take it and it would help reduce the number of drug addicts and alcoholics in deprived areas.

. . .

Once I made the decision to leave prostitution I started looking for another job. I got a job as a contract cleaner, and it suited me very well because it was only for three hours a day. I didn't have any references to give them, but once they saw I was a hard worker, there were never any problems. The money was bad compared to prostitution, but I learned to cut my cloth to suit my measure.

It was great to be able to work out of the cold; these days it doesn't matter if it is raining or snowing, I am indoors away from the elements. When I was working on the streets, my feet would be so cold when I'd come home I wouldn't be able to feel them.

I think it would help the women, though, if prostitution was legalised. It would do away with all the pimping and the men wouldn't be able to take over. If it was legalised, then it would be a safe house and the women would pay their taxes. It'll take time, but it might happen one day. At the end of the day, the women's safety is the priority. If I choose to work in prostitution, then it is the government's job to offer protection to me. If you're 21 or over then it should be classed as a job—because that's what it is. You don't enjoy it; you only do it for the money. Women who start working as prostitutes should be interviewed and asked why they want to sell themselves.

The government should open up some safe houses in different areas and five or six women could work in them. If the women ran it themselves, then it would get rid of the pimps. It would take away some of the stigma as well.

It would also protect the men, because if the women were taking health checks and had to get tested for AIDS every three months, it would stop the spread of the disease. The woman should be registered in a clinic and carry a card to show they are clean, like in Amsterdam and other countries.

If prostitution was legalised while I was working in it, I wouldn't have suffered the abuse, the rapes, and the beatings. I wouldn't have suffered the cold nights and the fear. I probably would have retired from prostitution earlier, but I would have a lot more options open to me if I wanted to stay in the business in some form or another.

epilogue

Even if prostitution was legalised tomorrow, I still wouldn't go back to it. I have a few business ideas that I got while working on the streets and there are some good ways of making money out of men's fantasies without working as a prostitute.

I'd love to open my own business in the 'baby born' area. It's a fetish some men have where they love to be dressed up as babies. I did some of it when I worked the streets—I'd give them bottles and put nappies on them. I'd have about five women working for me, and it would be totally within the law and above board, but obviously there would be need for discretion. There's good money to be made in it.

Another profession I'd like to get into would be counselling. I'd make a very good counsellor,

especially to other prostitutes because I can understand the suffering they go through. I know a
counsellor can't identify with everything, but I
learned to listen to a lot of problems when I worked
the streets and I'd never betray a secret. I am very
good at keeping things to myself and when you work
in the business, you learn to keep a lot of things secret
from a lot of people. I might do a course in
counselling when the time is right, and I'll know when
the time comes.

In the meantime I'm happy to continue working in
animal rescue. I'm still working as a cleaner, so I keep
myself busy. I spend a lot of time with my
grandchildren and I love meeting my friends for a few
drinks or a meal.

My life is a lot happier now since I've left the
streets. I'm a lot more content and at ease with myself.
I don't drink much. I sleep better at night. I don't have
to look over my shoulder the whole time and I don't
have to worry about getting murdered. I feel there's
more to me than just prostitution, so I look after
myself better.

My daughter is happier too. Sometimes prostitutes
forget how much they affect their family. Sometimes
people think if you're a prostitute then you're isolated
and on your own, but it's not always like that. Your
family worry about you—your sisters worry, your
brothers worry, your good friends worry.

I don't get the 'flu or pneumonia the way I used to. Every winter I would be laid low with the 'flu and problems with my breathing, but it hasn't happened since leaving the streets.

Some of the locals don't let me forget my past, but I know what went on in their past as well, and I'd rather have my past than theirs. They don't interest me. They're bigger whores because they slept with men just to get drink out of them, and some of them were married. I don't bother talking to women like that. Sometimes they try to get to me through my daughter, because she won't fight back. I didn't bring her up to be a fighter, so if anyone hits my daughter, then I beat them up. I don't let anyone touch her. What they seem to forget, is that I slept with men for money, but at least I got well paid. Some of the women who look down on prostitutes have questionable morals to say the least. There are women who work in offices and banks and they wouldn't sleep with someone if they didn't buy them drink, or get them jewellery or presents; so I don't see any difference between getting money for it or getting other rewards for it. It's usually the women who run other women down.

Sometimes I wonder if I was born to be a prostitute. Even when I was a child, men always sought me out. When I was playing in St. Stephen's Green the men would give me ten bob to feel me, then they found me when I was playing in the Phoenix Park. I knew about sex very young. I never played like a normal child. I never went to school much, because I was too tired, hungry and stressed to learn.

If I thought a child was going through what I went through, then I'd be the first one to call the police. If I thought a child was being abused either sexually or physically I'd make sure they were taken out of danger. I'm fanatical about children's safety, because I suffered so much myself.

Then I think about what life is like now. I've left the streets and I know I wasn't born to become a prostitute. Circumstances dictated I ended up working on the streets. I suppose it's the age old argument of nature versus nurture. I was nurtured towards becoming a prostitute and I'm lucky my nature allowed me to survive it. To survive prostitution doesn't simply mean walking away with your life. It means walking away with your mental health and your strong spirit. I was lucky I had a full life so I didn't feel the gap too much when I left prostitution.

I said earlier on that I was like two different people when I was working the streets. I'm happy to say that I left that 'night-time' side of me behind and I'm much calmer now. I'm still assertive and I can take care of myself, but I don't have the aggression in me that was necessary for my survival on the streets.

Most evenings after work I sit down in front of the television surrounded by my dogs, and have a cup of tea to relax. My grandchildren come in and out regularly and I have a wonderful home and family life.

Once upon a time I merely existed; now I'm living again.